mel bay presents

the flutist's companion

a comprehensive method

by mizzy mc caskill
and dona gilliam

"Before a man can produce anything great, he must understand the means by which he has to produce it."

Goethe

CONTENTS

REFERENCE

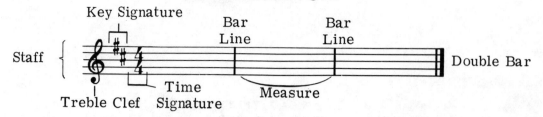

Time Signature

4 3 2 - Top number tells how many counts in a measure
4,4,4 - Bottom number tells what kind of note receives one count
(1/4 or one quarter note)

Notes and Rests

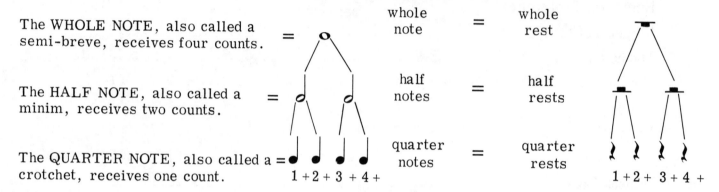

The WHOLE NOTE, also called a semi-breve, receives four counts.

The HALF NOTE, also called a minim, receives two counts.

The QUARTER NOTE, also called a crotchet, receives one count.

COMPOUND TIME

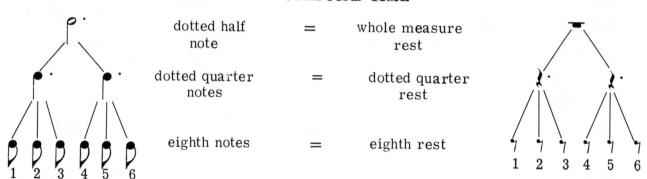

dotted half note = whole measure rest

dotted quarter notes = dotted quarter rest

eighth notes = eighth rest

Musical Symbols

♭ - A flat sign lowers a pitch 1/2 step

♯ - A sharp sign raises a pitch 1/2 step

♮ - A natural sign cancels a sharp or flat

♭♭ - A double flat lowers a pitch one whole step

𝄪 - A double sharp raises a pitch one whole step

Accidentals affect only tones within that octave within that measure.

Musical Terms

Dynamics

DYNAMIC markings indicate the degree of loudness and softness to be used when playing.

cresc. or ◁————— . . . . crescendo...gradually getting louder

decresc. or —————▷ . . . . decrescendo or
                                    diminuendo...gradually getting softer

ff . . . . fortissimo...very loud

f . . . . forte...loud

mf . . . . mezzo-forte...moderately loud

mp . . . . mezzo-piano...moderately soft

p . . . . piano...softly

pp . . . . pianissimo...very soft

Tempo

TEMPO markings indicate the rate of speed at which a composition is to be played.

Accelerando (accel.) . . . . growing faster
Adagio . . . . slowly, leisurely
Allegretto . . . . lively; faster than andante, slower than allegro
Allegro . . . . lively and fast
Andante . . . . moderately slow
Assai . . . . very
Grave . . . . very slow and solemn
Larghetto . . . . a little faster than Largo
Largo . . . . slow, broad, and stately
Lento . . . . slow; between andante and largo
Meno Mosso . . . . less motion; slower
Moderato . . . . a moderate speed
Presto . . . . very fast; faster than allegro
Tempo di Valse . . . . waltz tempo
Vivace . . . . brisk, lively, fast

Style

STYLE markings indicate the manner in which a piece is to be played.

Animato . . . . with spirit
A tempo . . . . in the original tempo
Dolce . . . . sweetly
Espressivo . . . . expressively
Grandioso . . . . in a grand manner
Legato . . . . smoothly, connected
Leggiero . . . . lightly
Maestoso . . . . majestic and dignified
Marcato . . . . marked, and with emphasis
Non troppo . . . . not too much
Poco . . . . little
Rall. (rallentando) . . . . gradually getting slower
Rit. (ritardando) . . . . gradually getting slower
Simile . . . . similarly; in a like manner
Staccato . . . . separated, detached
Tenuto . . . . held out to full value

MAJOR/MINOR SCALES

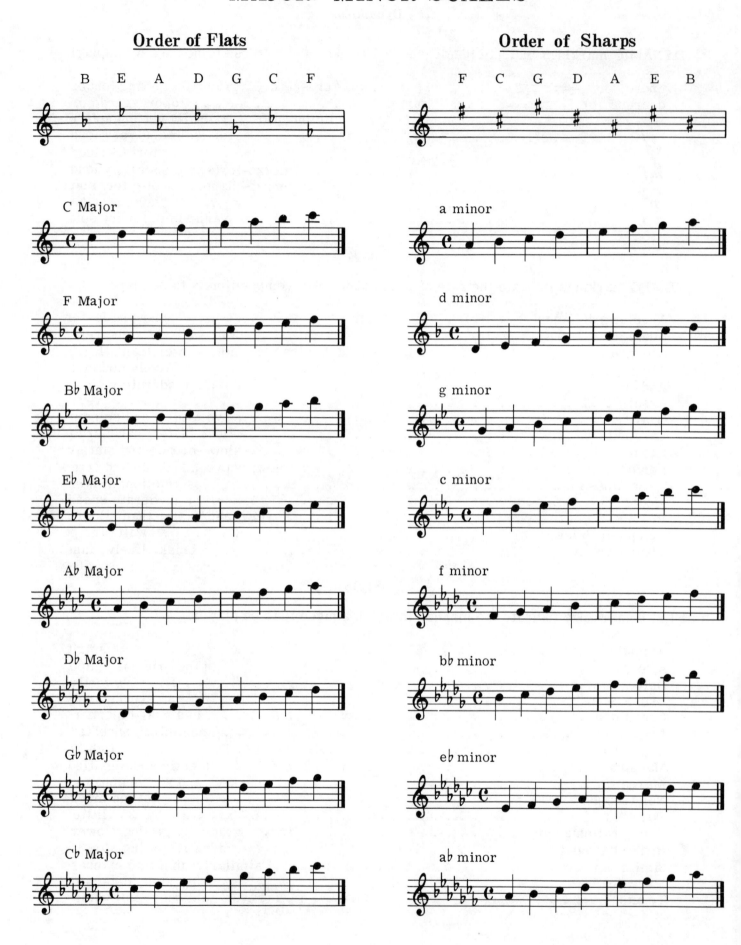

G Major

e minor

D Major

b minor

A Major

f# minor

E Major

c# minor

B Major

g# minor

F# Major

d# minor

C# Major

a# minor

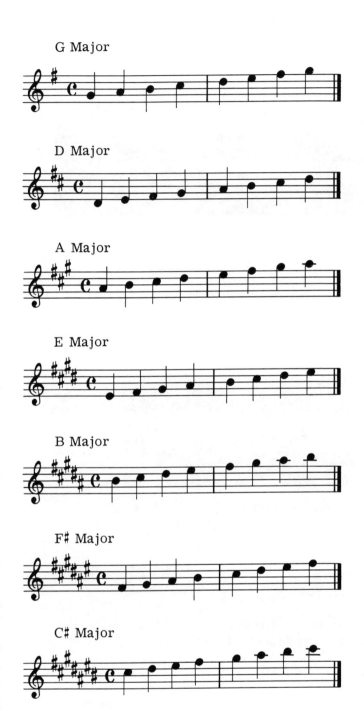
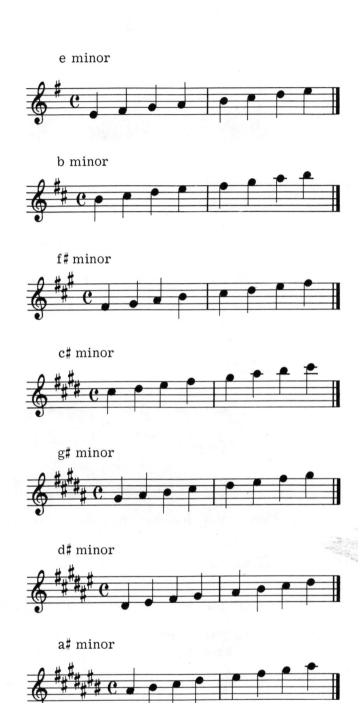

ASSEMBLY/CARE

Assembling and Dismantling:

head joint   body

                                                                    foot joint

- Gently twist joints together or apart.

- Avoid crushing delicate key mechanisms.

- When assembling, leave the headjoint pulled out approximately 1/8" for tuning
  purposes.

Alignment:

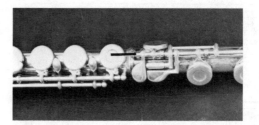

Center of embouchure hole with first key   Middle of last key to rod of foot joint

Flute Care:

- After playing, swab each joint clean with a soft cloth.

- Wipe finger prints and moisture off of key mechanism and outside of instrument.
  Avoid rubbing keys in a circular motion as this will damage the mechanism.

- Keep pads dry. To remove excess moisture blot pads with cigarette paper or lens tissue.

- Cork placement should be 17mm from the center of the embouchure hole. Periodically
  check with mark on cleaning rod and adjust accordingly.

- Once or twice a year, oil the key mechanism with fine grade key oil or clock oil.
  Apply a tiny drop of key oil wherever one metal part moves against another.
  Carefully dab off any excess oil.

HAND POSITION/BALANCE/POSTURE

<u>Left Hand Position:</u> Flute rests on the first joint of left index finger.
Thumb operates the B and B flat keys on the backside.

<u>Right Hand Position:</u> Thumb lies beneath first two fingers of the right hand.
Little finger rests on the E flat key.

Note: Fingers remain close to keys to provide maximum technical efficiency with
minimal movement.

Support and Balance Points

A. Support
   1. r.h. thumb
   2. first joint of left
      index finger
B. Balance
   1. lower lip
   2. r.h. little finger

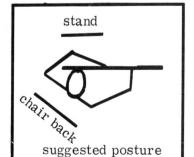

stand

chair back
suggested posture

Posture

Whether sitting or standing good posture is a
necessity for proper breath support. Correct
posture should allow for an unrestricted column
of air as well as comfortable arm and shoulder
position.

EMBOUCHURE/BREATH CONTROL

Embouchure (ahm - ba - shur): formation of lips in playing position

Due to variations in lip and mouth formation there is not one correct embouchure.

Formation of embouchure:
1. Use a mirror. Rest lower lip on embouchure plate. The embouchure plate rests in the natural indentation of the jaw.

2. The edge of the embouchure hole should be against the edge of the lower lip (approximately where the red meets the white).

3. Stretch the lips back as if to smile (sardonically) while simultaneously forming a tiny opening as if to whistle (stretch back and pucker forward).

4. The resulting aperture should form an ellipse ◯ that is centered over the embouchure hole.

Lower lip should cover 1/4 to 1/3 of the embouchure hole, and as much of the plate from side to side as possible.

Keep lips parallel to embouchure plate.

5. Blow a focused airstream partly into and partly across the embouchure hole. Split the airstream over the far edge of the hole (backwall).

6. Roll headjoint in or out to find the angle where the most resonant tone is produced.

    Variations in this basic embouchure are possible. The key is to form an embouchure that is flexible. It must allow the production of a well focused and controlled sound over all registers from soft, clear highs to full-bodied lows.

Breath Control:

    Good tone production begins with proper breathing and posture. Good breath control requires regulated and prolonged exhalation. This entails the use of the diaphragm*, intercostal (chest), and abdominal muscles acting together to create proper support for the airstream.

To inhale correctly:

    - inhale quickly, deeply, through the mouth
    - keep throat open and relaxed (avoid noise caused by a constricted windway)
    - fill lungs from the bottom up
    - let the stomach expand (diaphragm flattens and allows more air to enter chest cavity)
    - keep the shoulders from rising

To exhale correctly:

    - gradually relax the diaphragm while adding pressure with the abdominal and intercostal muscles
    - tension thusly created between abdominal and intercostal muscles (called breath support) allows for control over speed and amount of air released

Following is an exercise to encourage proper support and breath control:

    - lie on back and rest a heavy object on abdomen
    -push the weight up quickly as you inhale
    - suspend for a moment, then, exhale slowly and evenly keeping muscles firm as object descends

* Diaphragm - wall of connective tissues and muscles separating the chest cavity from the abdominal cavity

HEADJOINT/ARTICULATION

<u>Articulation</u>: Articulation is the pronunciation of a musical sound which involves the starting, duration, and release of the sound.

Start: A tone is started when air pressure is released by the tongue. The tip of the tongue should be placed on the gum behind the upper teeth and released as if whispering the syllable "too" or "tah". Avoid using vocal sounds when articulating.

Duration: As long as a tone is sustained the tongue should stay relaxed and out of the way of the airstream.

Release: Release a tone with the breath, not the tongue. Avoid "tut" articulations.

To establish a beginning tone use the headjoint alone.

- Hold end of headjoint with left hand
- Close open end with palm of right hand

Headjoint Exercise

1. Set embouchure (a mirror is extremely useful)
2. Build air pressure behind tongue
3. Release air with the tongue and blow steady stream
4. End the tone by stopping the breath

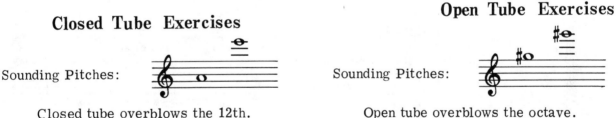

Closed Tube Exercises

Sounding Pitches:

Closed tube overblows the 12th.

Open Tube Exercises

Sounding Pitches:

Open tube overblows the octave.

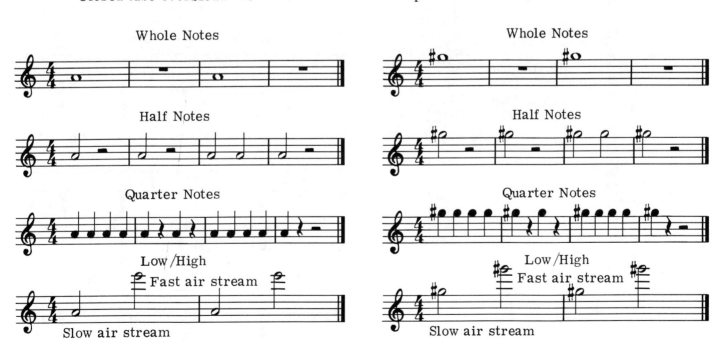

FINGERING CHART

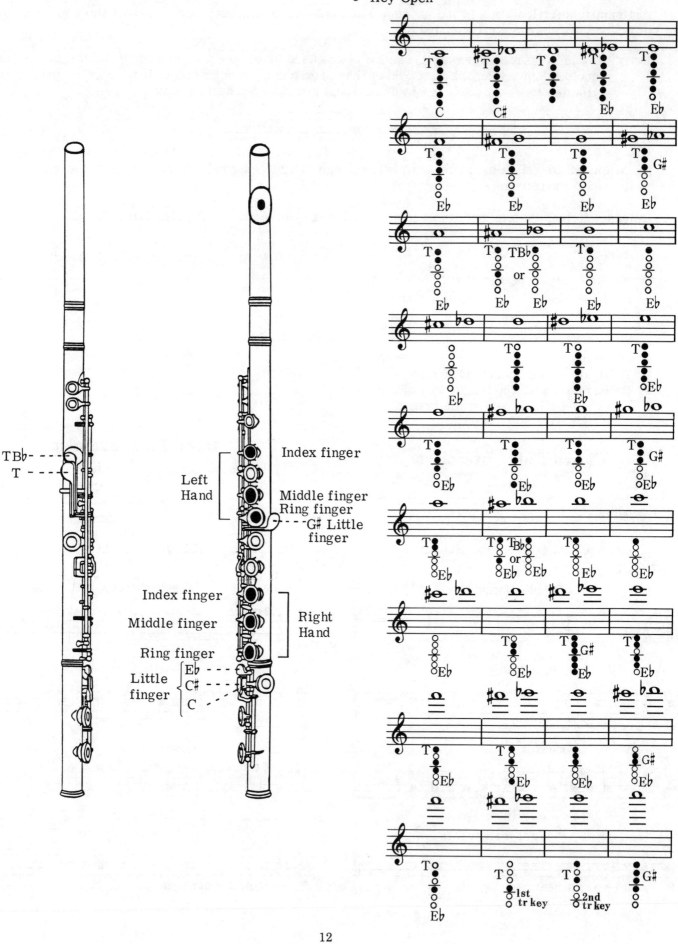

LONG TONE STUDY

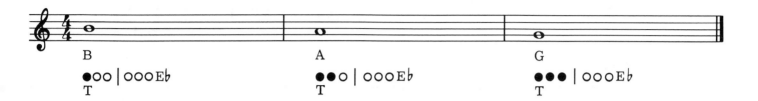

Whole Note Exercise

Half Note Exercise

Quarter Note Exercise

REPEAT SIGNS

REPEAT SIGNS indicate that music between the two signs is to be repeated. If only one repeat sign is used return to the beginning.

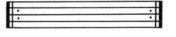

Finger Exercise

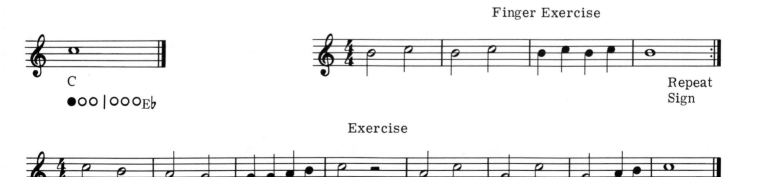

Repeat Sign

Exercise

SLURS⁄DOTTED HALF NOTE

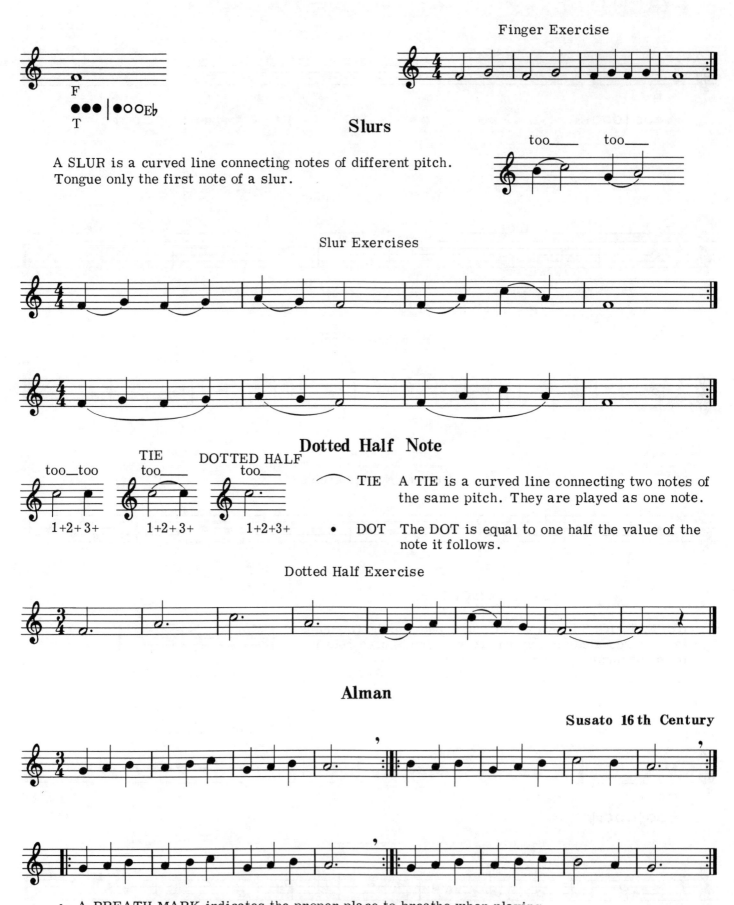

Finger Exercise

Slurs

A SLUR is a curved line connecting notes of different pitch. Tongue only the first note of a slur.

too___ too___

Slur Exercises

Dotted Half Note

TIE   A TIE is a curved line connecting two notes of the same pitch. They are played as one note.

DOT   The DOT is equal to one half the value of the note it follows.

Dotted Half Exercise

Alman

Susato 16th Century

, -A BREATH MARK indicates the proper place to breathe when playing.

14

OCTAVE STUDY

To Play Upper Octave Notes:

 * use faster air stream
 * blow more across embouchure hole
 * make aperture smaller

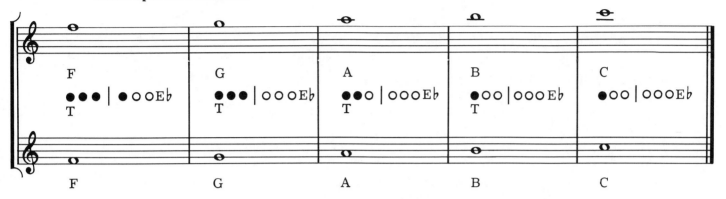

Octave Exercises

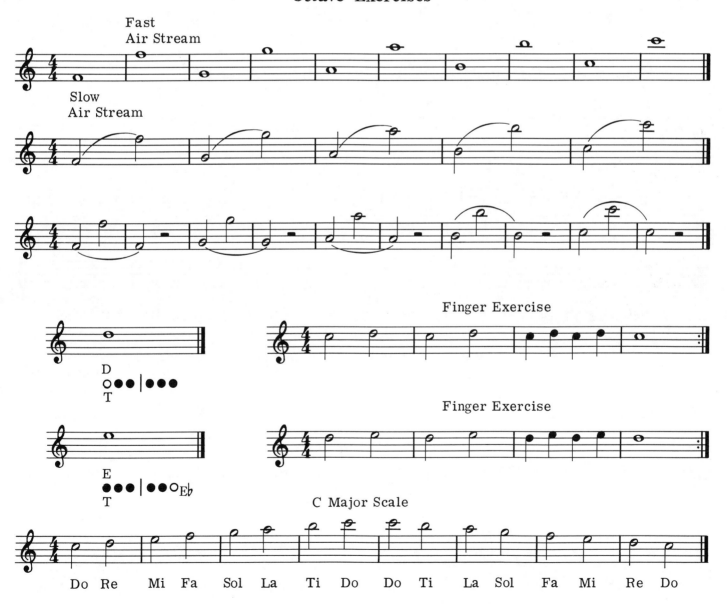

F MAJOR STUDY

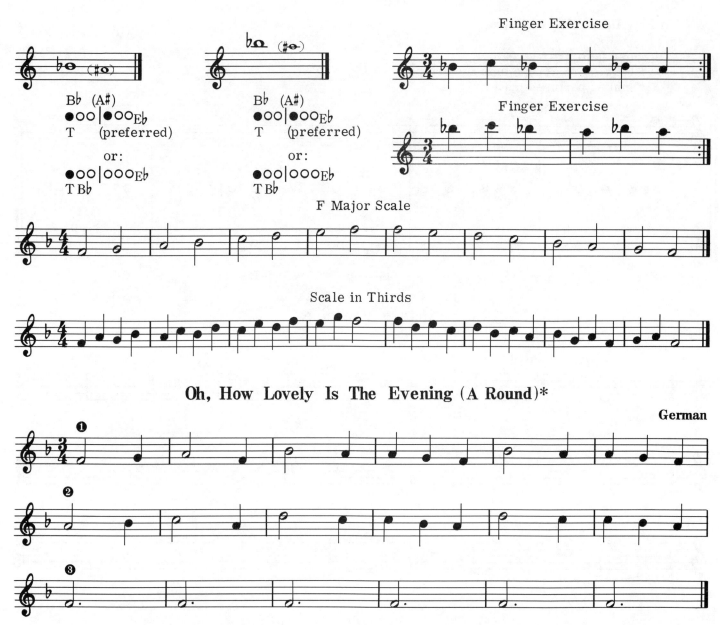

Finger Exercise

Bb (A#)
●○○|●○○Eb
T (preferred)

or:
●○○|○○○Eb
T Bb

Bb (A#)
●○○|●○○Eb
T (preferred)

or:
●○○|○○○Eb
T Bb

Finger Exercise

F Major Scale

Scale in Thirds

Oh, How Lovely Is The Evening (A Round)*

German

* A ROUND is a song in which two or more groups play the same melody starting at different times.

Sumer Is Icumen In (A Canon)*

Old English

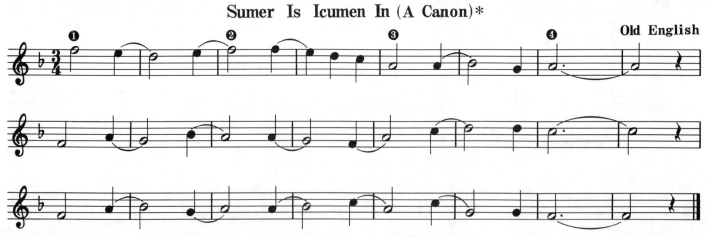

* Similar to a ROUND is a CANON, in which each voice imitates the original melody at different times.

G MAJOR STUDY

Finger Exercise

Finger Exercise

F#   Gb

F#   Gb

G Major Scale

Scale in Thirds

Riddle Song

Here is a piece beginning on the last count of a measure.
This note is called a pick-up note.

Traditional

Exercise

Exercise

17

EIGHTH NOTE STUDY

The EIGHTH NOTE, also called a quaver, receives one half of a count and is written with one flag or connecting bar.

The EIGHTH REST receives one half of a count and is written with one flag.

Eighth Note Exercise

Eighth Rest Exercise

The Ashgrove

Traditional

Minuet

Moderato

Rameau

D MAJOR STUDY

Finger Exercise

Finger Exercise

Exercise

Finger Exercise

D Major Scale

Scale in Thirds

Hampton Court

Weideman

Minuet

J.S. Bach

Sonatina

Beethoven

STACCATO AND TENUTO

A STACCATO mark means to play in a separated and detached manner.

A TENUTO mark means to play notes to their fullest value.

SIMILE means to continue playing in a similar style.

Menuet

Allegro moderato

Corrette

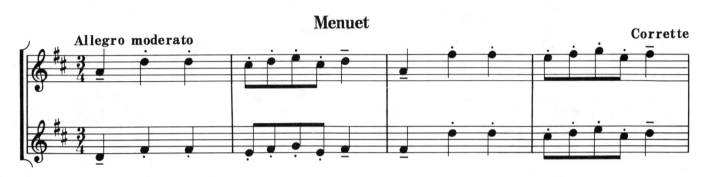

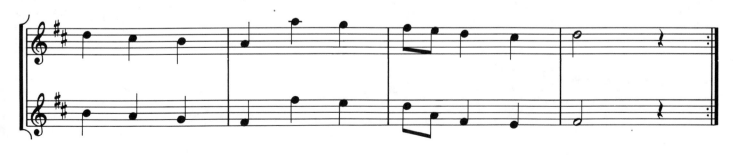

Duet #1

F. Meline

DOTTED QUARTER NOTE STUDY

Dotted Quarter Exercise

Lovely Joan

Traditional

Simple Gifts

Shaker Hymn

Barbara Allen

Scottish

Cockles and Mussels

Irish

B FLAT MAJOR STUDY

E FLAT MAJOR STUDY

D.C. al Fine - Da Capo al Fine means to repeat from the beginning to a place marked Fine.

25

A MAJOR STUDY

A Major Scale

Scale in Thirds

Duet

Hotteterre

27

SIXTEENTH NOTES

The SIXTEENTH NOTE receives one fourth of a count and is written with two flags or two connecting bars.

The SIXTEENTH REST receives one fourth of a count and is written with two flags.

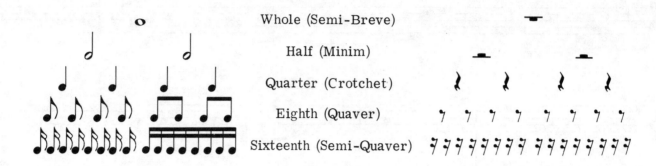

Whole (Semi-Breve)
Half (Minim)
Quarter (Crotchet)
Eighth (Quaver)
Sixteenth (Semi-Quaver)

Exercises

The Rakes of Mallow

Irish

Finale to Inkle and Yarico

from Evening Amusement (1796)

28

Exercise in F*

*Use thumb B♭

G. Rabboni

Exercise in E Flat

R.S. Pratten

Murray's Hornpipe

Irish

D.S. al Fine - Dal Segno al Fine means to go back to the sign 𝄋 and play to Fine (End).

Jim Boulton's Fancy

DOTTED EIGHTH NOTE STUDY

Dotted Eighth Exercise

Country Gardens

English Folk Song

Captain Mackintosh's March

from The Fifer's Companion, 1805

TRIPLET STUDY

A TRIPLET is a group of three notes played in the time of two notes of the same value. They are indicated by a figure 3 and usually a slur which is placed over or under the group of three notes.

Triplet Exercise

Grano's March

from The Compleat Tutor for the
German Flute (1765)

Sailor's Delight

Traditional

CHROMATIC SCALE STUDY

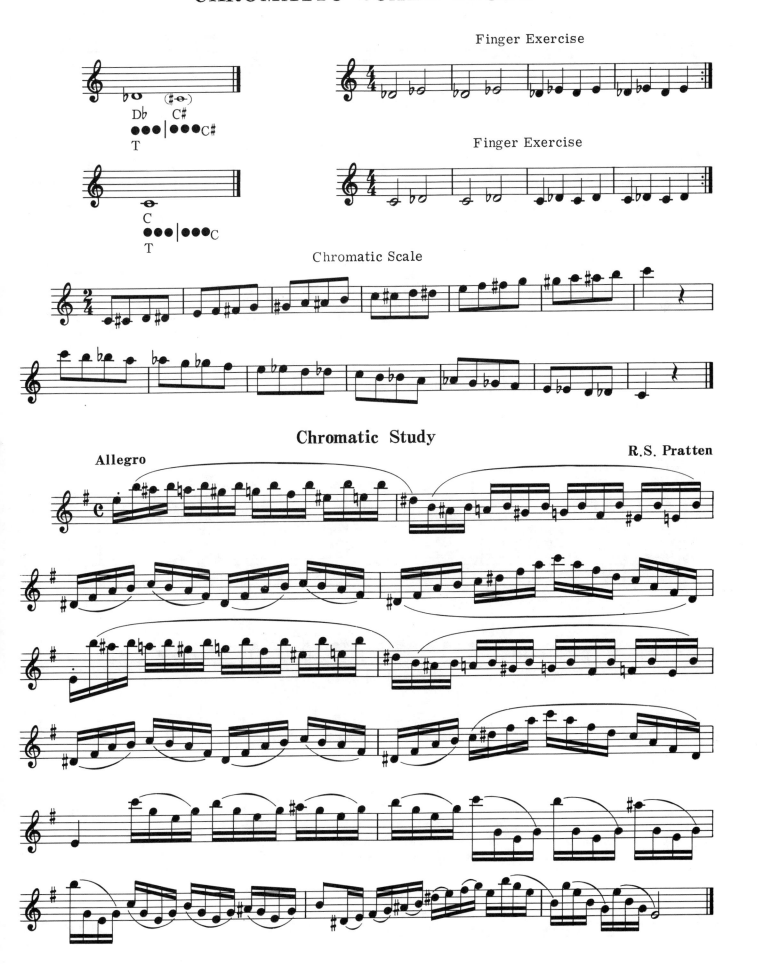

Finger Exercise

Finger Exercise

Chromatic Scale

Chromatic Study

Allegro

R.S. Pratten

Finger Exercise

Finger Exercise

D Major Scale

Syncopation

SYNCOPATION is the accenting of a weak beat.

Devienne

Duet

Devienne

COMPOUND TIME

COMPOUND TIME SIGNATURES are those in which the strong counts are subdivided by three.

Counted in six: 1   2   3   4   5   6
Counted in two: 1   -   -   2   -   -
$\frac{6}{8}$ is the compound of $\frac{2}{4}$

Counted in nine: 1 2 3 4 5 6 7 8 9
Counted in three: 1 - - 2 - - 3 - -
$\frac{9}{8}$ is the compound of $\frac{3}{4}$

Take It Easy (Double Jig)

Irish

Sonata in F, Op. 1, No. 11

G.F. Handel

Allegro

35

Exercise

R.S. Pratten

Exercise

R.S. Pratten

Waltzer

from Riley's Flute Melodies (1820)

The Idle Road

Irish

MINOR KEY STUDY

For every major scale there is a relative minor scale with the same key signature.
The relative minor of C Major is A minor.

Exercise in A Minor

Sonata No. 4 (Adagio Movement)

Marcello

MINOR KEY STUDY

G Major   E Minor

Exercise in E Minor

D Major   B Minor

Exercise in B Minor

Exercise in F# Minor

Exercise in D Minor

B♭ Major

G Minor

Exercise in G Minor

E♭ Major

C Minor

Exercise in C Minor

E FLAT MAJOR STUDY

Finger Exercise

E♭ G# D#   E♭   D#   E♭   D#
●●●|●●●E♭   ○●●●|●●●E♭   ●●●|●●●E♭
T   T   T

E Flat Major Scale

Etude

Etude

E MAJOR STUDY

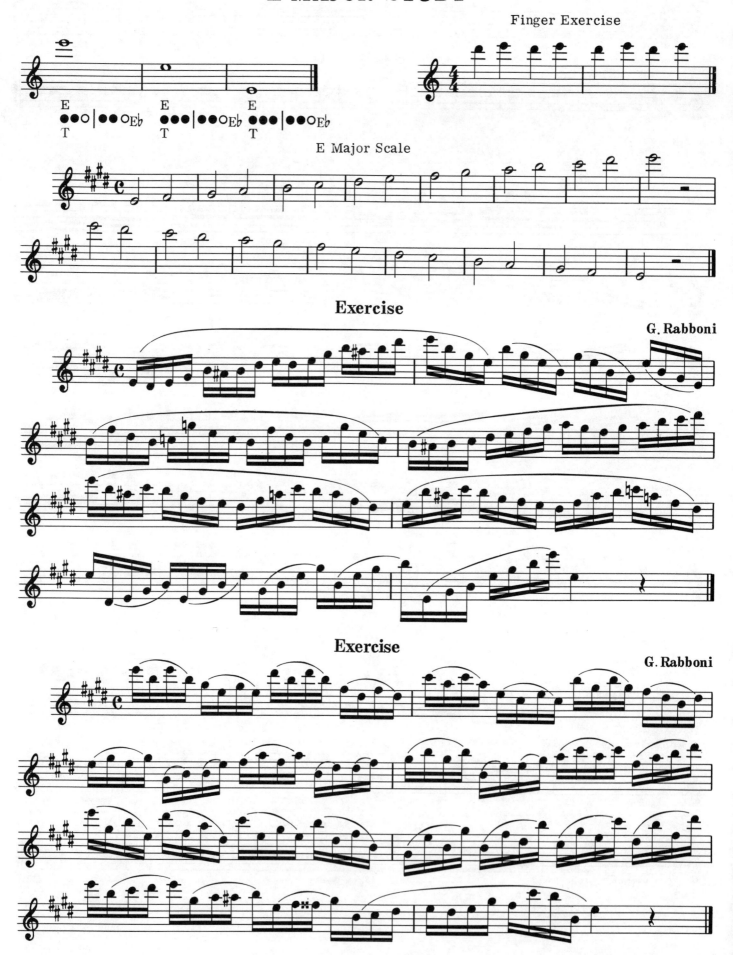

Finger Exercise

E Major Scale

Exercise

G. Rabboni

Exercise

G. Rabboni

F MAJOR STUDY

Finger Exercise

F Major Scale

Study No. 7

R.S. Pratten

Allegro moderato

G MAJOR STUDY

Finger Exercise

Finger Exercise

G Major Scale

Exercise

Exercise

R.S. Pratten

A FLAT MAJOR STUDY

Finger Exercise

A Flat Major Scale

Etude

Lindpainter

Allegro

HIGH REGISTER STUDY

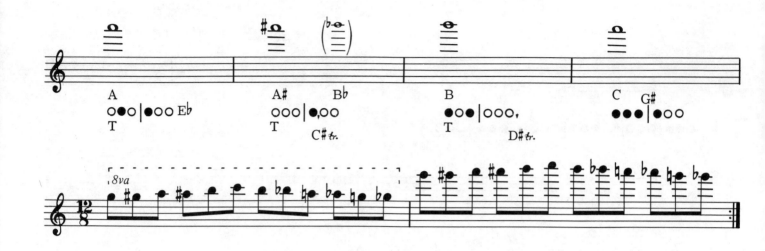

Three Octave Chromatic Scale

High Register Studies

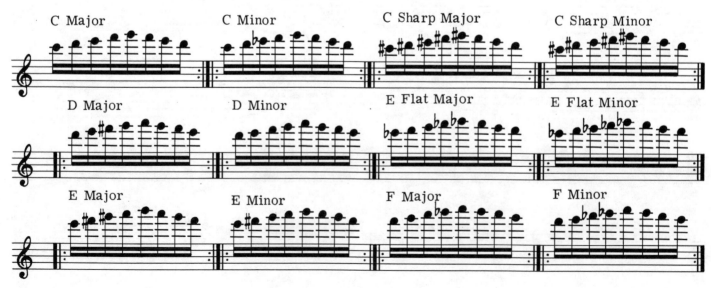

Octave Study

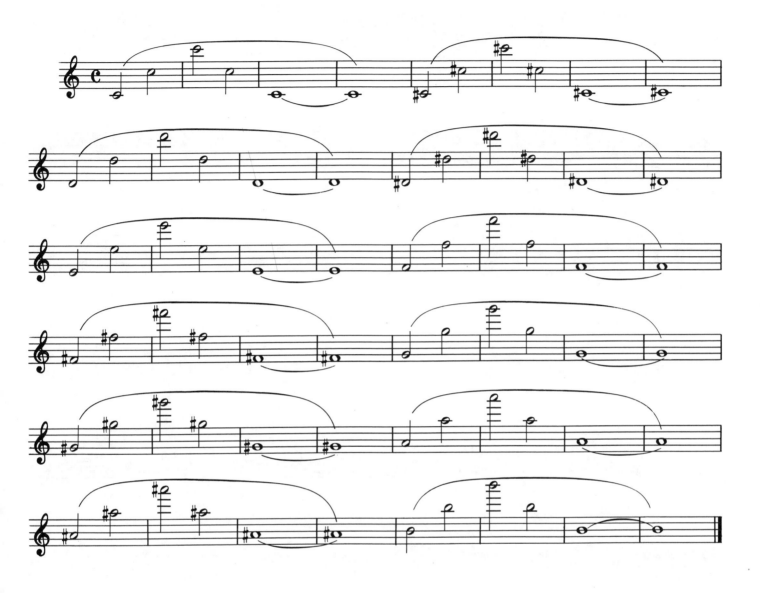

Five Note Scale Patterns

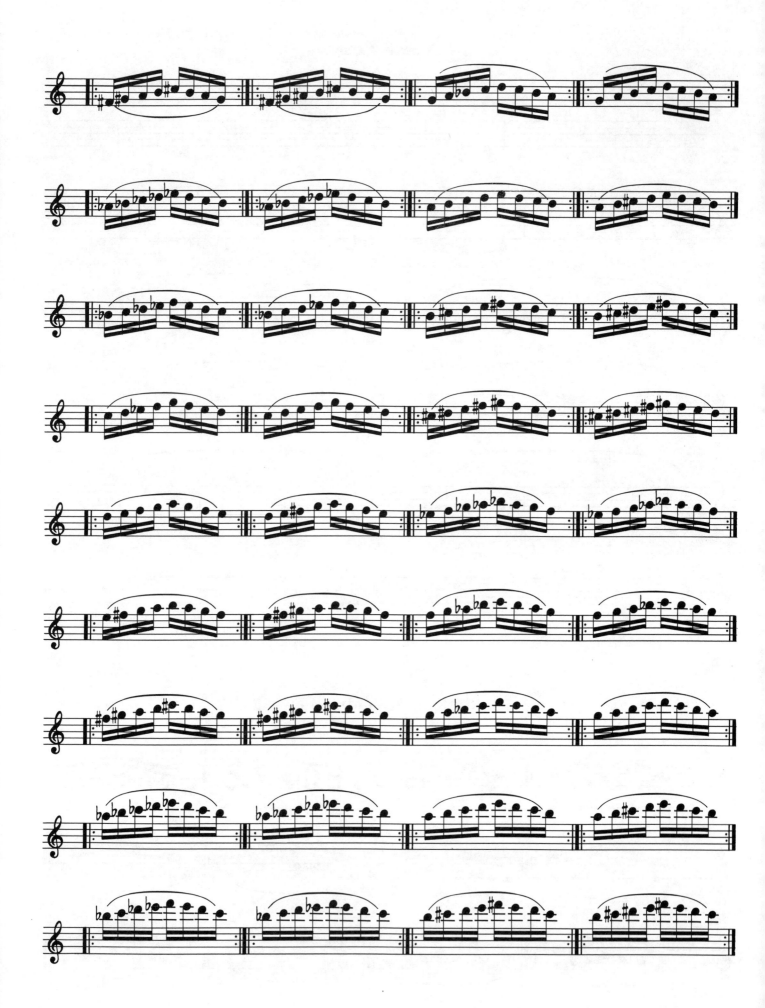

48

49

OCTAVE STUDY

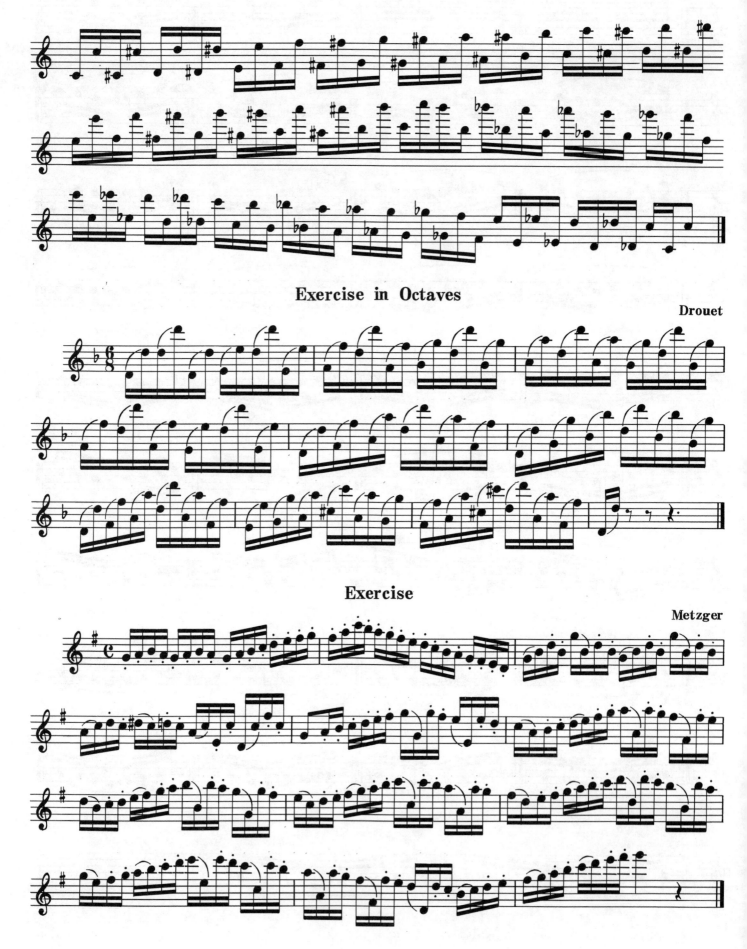

Exercise in Octaves

Drouet

Exercise

Metzger

DOUBLE TONGUING

Double tonguing is a multiple articulation pattern used when playing fast passages. This tonguing procedure alternates the syllables "tu" and "ku" or "doo" and "goo" in rapid succession. e.g.

tu	ku	tu	ku	tu	ku	tu	ku
doo	goo	doo	goo	doo	goo	doo	goo
ta	ka	ta	ka	ta	ka	ta	ka
ti	ki	ti	ki	ti	ki	ti	ki
teh	keh	teh	keh	teh	keh	teh	keh

Although this may be cumbersome at first, careful practice emphasizing evenness of the second syllable will allow fast passages to be played with ease.

Exercise

Study

51

TRIPLE TONGUING

Similar to double tonguing is triple tonguing, a multiple articulation pattern used in fast passages where there are groupings of three notes.

There are two basic alternation patterns used in triple tonguing:

Exercise

Exercise

TRILLS

The TRILL marked *tr* or *tr*⌇ is played by rapidly alternating the written note with the next note above
or
(Shake)
it in the scale.

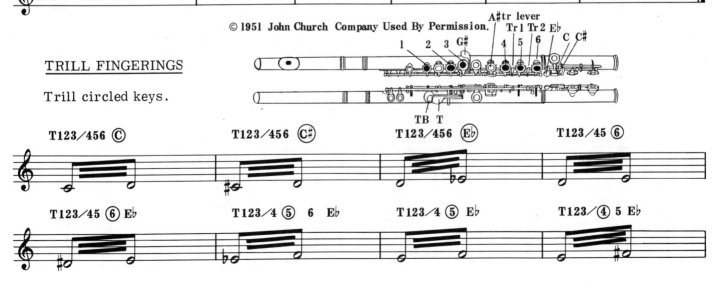

Stars and Stripes Forever

Sousa

© 1951 John Church Company Used By Permission.

<u>TRILL FINGERINGS</u>

Trill circled keys.

53

TRILL FINGERINGS

Trill circled keys.

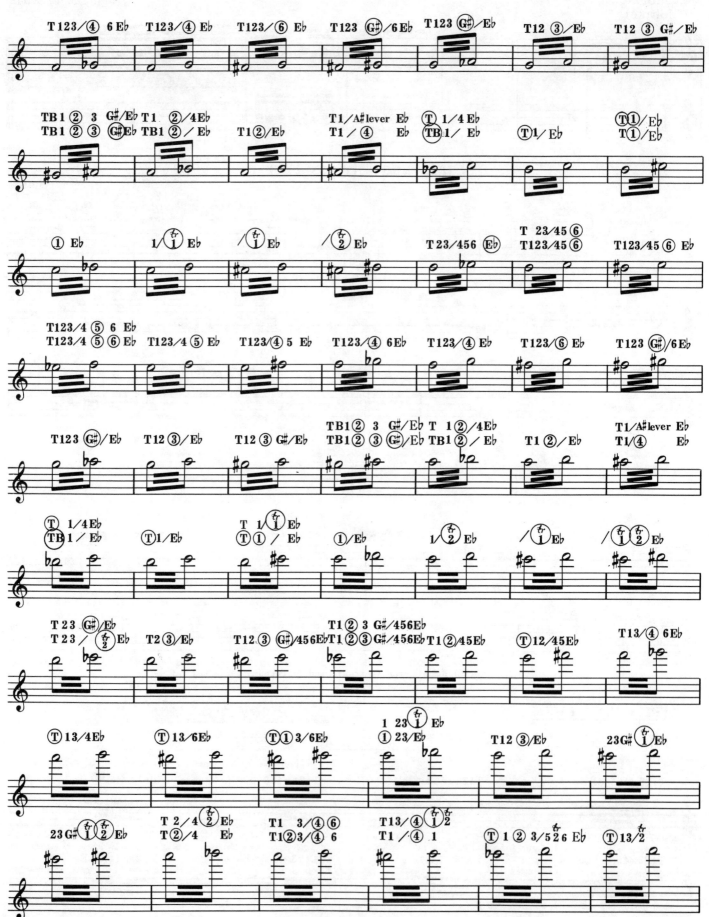

54

Whole Step Trill Exercise

Half Step Trill Exercise

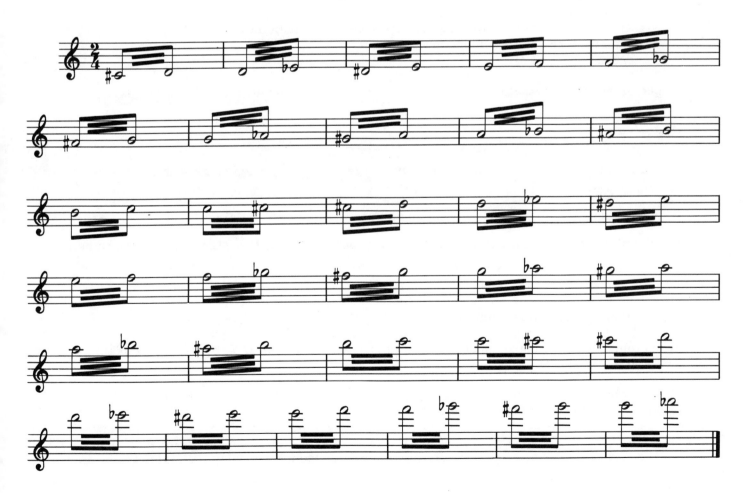

INTONATION

Common to all flutes are certain pitch irregularities. Intonation precision and accuracy will only come through listening to harmonic and intervallic relationships. The table given below references the Boehm flute and is a starting point from which to work.

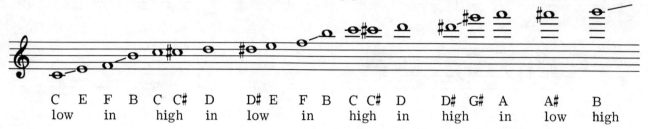

C	E	F	B	C	C#	D	D#	E	F	B	C	C#	D	D#	G#	A	A#	B
low	in	high	in	low		in	high		in		low	in		high		in	low	high

NOTE: Scales and tunings vary among different instrument makers (see p. 107).

To stabilize relative pitch a proper warm-up is necessary

- when the instrument is <u>cold</u> the tendency is to be <u>flat</u>
- when the instrument is <u>hot</u> the tendency is to be <u>sharp</u>

To <u>LOWER</u> pitch

- pull headjoint out
- angle airstream more into the embouchure hole (roll headjoint in)
- make aperture larger (drop jaw, relax embouchure)
- decrease speed of air

To <u>RAISE</u> pitch

- push headjoint in
- angle airstream across the embouchure hole (roll headjoint out)
- make aperture smaller (move jaw forward)
- increase speed of air

The player must compensate for pitch changes in crescendo and diminuendo passages.

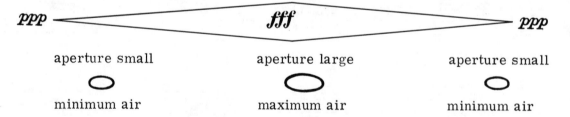

aperture small	aperture large	aperture small
minimum air	maximum air	minimum air

Practice pitch stabilization and accuracy on long tones. Work with a stroboscope may be helpful.

Tuning

- Warm up properly before tuning

- When tuning with the piano, sound the flute tone first so as not to be biased by the piano (use the A registers).

- When tuning with flutes or other instruments, stabilize one tone as a reference and let another player smooth the tone (remove the beats).

Beats: Variations in loudness heard when two tones (one of slightly higher frequency) are sounded simultaneously. The greater the difference in frequency the faster the beats.

HARMONICS

A complex flute tone consists of many pure tones called harmonics. The lowest harmonic is called the fundamental frequency, and it determines the pitch of a tone. Components of the harmonic series may also be called overtones* or partials*. It is the relative strengths (amplitude) of these partials in the complex tone which give instruments their characteristic tone qualities (timbre).

*<u>Partial</u> - Any component of the harmonic series including the fundamental.
*<u>Overtone</u> - One of the frequencies produced by the complex tone. All overtones are higher than the fundamental frequency and a whole number multiple of it. The fundamental is not an overtone.

Given below is a series of harmonics which may be played by overblowing the fundamental frequency C.

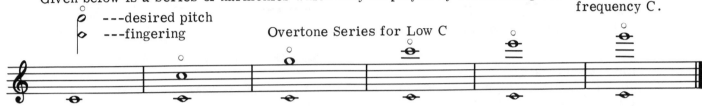

Theoretically the harmonic series continues upward through the sound spectrum much higher than the human ear can perceive. The higher the harmonic the more difficult it is to isolate and sustain.

Overtone Series

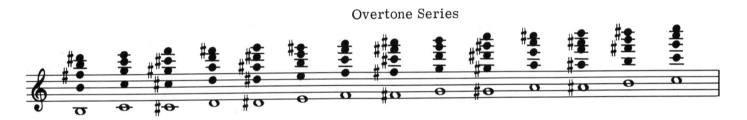

Taps

Reveille

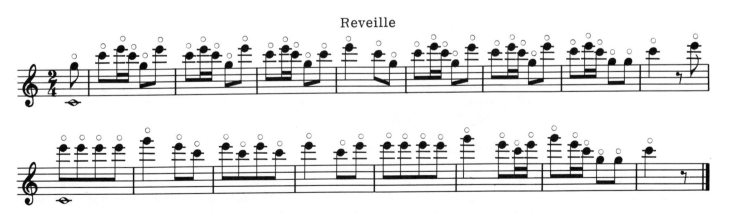

Practice <u>Taps</u> and <u>Reveille</u> on other fundamental frequencies.

HARMONICS/WHISTLE TONES

Upper Register Control

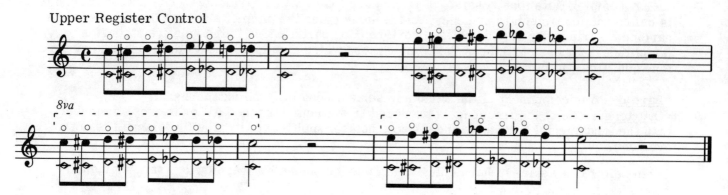

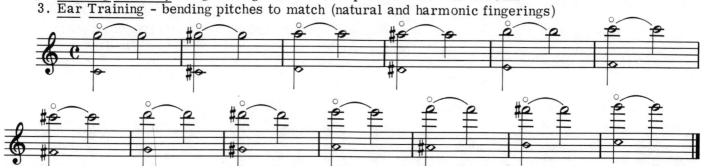

The following exercise aids in the development of:

1. <u>Embouchure Flexibility</u> - higher register notes require movement of the jaw forward to minimize aperture
2. <u>Blowing Intensity</u> - higher register notes require a faster air stream
3. <u>Ear Training</u> - bending pitches to match (natural and harmonic fingerings)

Why use harmonics?
- for their distinctive tone quality
- as alternative fingerings in difficult passages
- to develop control of embouchure and blowing intensity for accurate placement of tones in the upper register
- comparing intonation differences between regular and harmonic fingerings leads to a better understanding of acoustical properties of the instrument

Whistle Tones

Whistle tones, also called 'whisper tones' are soft, high, edge tones produced at very low dynamic levels.

Whistle tones may be used: - to completely relax the embouchure
- to aid in lip flexibility
- to control breath support

Production:
* Relax lips
* Begin the sound with the breath only
* Blow a small, steady stream of air across the embouchure hole
* Use minimal yet even breath pressure

Note: For best results use a mirror to properly focus the airstream. Condensation of breath should occur in an elliptical shape on the embouchure plate.

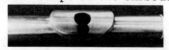

Condensation pattern

To gain control over breath support practice extended whistle tones. Strive to isolate and sustain each tone. The slightest change in breath support will cause an adjacent overtone to sound. Although whistle tones are rarely used in traditional literature, new techniques of amplification allow their sonorities to be greatly enhanced. Through amplification the door is opened to compositional techniques which exploit this additional sonority.

TONE STUDIES

Control of pitch and dynamics through tone drives:

Purpose: To increase or decrease loudness (amplitude) while sustaining constant pitch (frequency)

Factors controlling pitch and dynamics:

* Diaphragmatic pressure and velocity of airstream
    - a slower airstream lowers pitch
    - a faster airstream raises pitch

* Aperture
    - when playing p use a small aperture
    - when playing f use a large aperture

Tone Drives

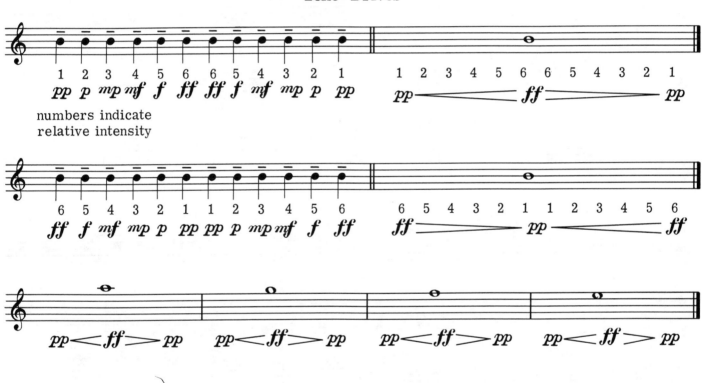

numbers indicate
relative intensity

Continue tone drives throughout the entire range of the instrument.

* practice with continuous sound and legato articulation

* for refinement of dynamic control experiment with air velocity, lip aperture, and the angle of the airstream

* daily practice of tone drives is imperative for interpreting a musical line

TONE STUDIES

* Equalize and blend the tone color throughout each register.
* Center (focus) each tone. Strive for maximum resonance.
* Use legato articulations.
* Change notes precisely. Concentrate on even finger movement.
* Maintain consistant breath support and precise intonation.

VIBRATO

One of the most common avenues of expression which a flutist uses is the vibrato. Vibrato is the pulsation of a tone used to add color and motion to a musical line. It involves the fluctuation of a tone's frequency (pitch), amplitude (loudness), and timbre (overtones). Although vibrato adds beauty to a tone its overuse may detract from a performance, therefore it must be used with discretion.

The prerequisite for using vibrato is a clear, steady sound where the throat is open and relaxed in all registers. If vibrato does not occur naturally it can be taught by controlling movement of air with the diaphragm, abdominal, and intercostal muscles.

METHOD:
* In the beginning it may be helpful to have a friend push against your abdomen to achieve rhythmic pulsation
* Start pulsations slowly with exaggerated motion, surging air as if pronouncing "hah"
* Use a metronome to regulate pulsations
* Evenly increase the speed of pulsations until they reach a comfortable rate
  (range of 2 to 9 per second to gain control of pulsations)
  (range of 5 to 9 per second most common in musical context)
* As the rate of vibrato increases the throat will begin interacting in the process.
  Note that diaphragmatic pulsations are stressed at first to avoid throat tension.

* As vibrato is learned it should be added without the conscious effort of the performer and at various speeds to fit the musical context.
* The speed of pulsations should be graduated throughout the range of the instrument with the lower register requiring a slower, wider vibrato and the higher register requiring a faster, narrower one.
* Practice control of vibrato in the following four dimensions:

  1. change the rate from slower to faster

  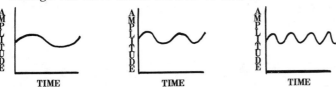

  2. change the amplitude from lesser to greater

  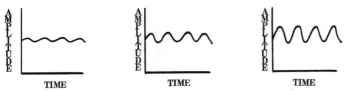

  3. change the vibrato during the course of a note

  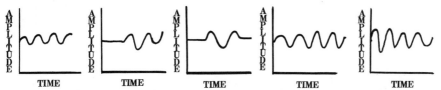

  4. play a tone without vibrato

Practice control of vibrato using the following pieces:

Greensleeves

Traditional

Sonata No. II in E♭ Major
(Siciliano)

Bach

Siciliano

TONE STUDIES

TONE COLORING: Adding expression while developing more than one basic sound on the flute is done through tone coloring (the changing of tone quality or timbre).

Factors affecting Tone Quality, Timbre, and Color are:

* Mechanics of the individual player
    - intensity/velocity of airstream created by breath support
    - angle of airstream as it strikes the backwall
    - shape and size of aperture
    - amount of embouchure hole covered by lower lip
    - vowel formation of mouth cavity
    - relaxation and openness of the throat

* Acoustics of the flute
    - size, shape, and taper of the bore
    - density of the material
    - cut of the embouchure hole and tone holes

EXTREMES OF COLORING:

* Dark, Hollow Sound, Pure Tone - strong fundamental with few overtones
    - use large aperture
    - minimal breath pressure to assure pitch
    - vowel formation of mouth cavity as "oh" or "ah"

* Bright, Brilliant, Complex Tone - more overtones present
    - use small aperture
    - intense breath pressure "think of projecting the tone"
    - vowel formation of mouth cavity from "oo" (loot) to "a" (day) to "e" (easy)

A good basic sound is achieved by striking a balance between the extremes. The maximum coloring possibilities are found in the low register where a more complete overtone series is present. The speed of vibrato is the main source of coloring in the upper octaves.

Experiment with manipulation of tone colors using the following melody.

Christ Child Lullaby

Gaelic

INTERPRETATION/PHRASING

Music is analogous to language in that it is a codified means of expression. As with any other means of communication music has formal structures which can be divided into smaller units or phrases. A phrase or musical idea is like a sentence. The manner in which we speak (articulate) and place emphasis on each word (note) determines how others will interpret what we say.

There are no absolute rules for the interpretation of a musical phrase as it is largely a matter of individual taste. There are, however, guidelines that can be followed:

1) Determine stylistic influences. Practice the appropriate techniques demanded for interpretation in that particular style: e.g. Baroque - ornamentation, Avant-Garde - new sonorities, extended techniques.

2) Define the melodic lines through analysis of the underlying harmonic structure, and wherever possible plot breath marks in accordance with cadence points. Note the contour of the lines with their rising and/or falling intensities from climax to resolution. The contour will indicate the most expressive points within the line.

1)

2)

Dynamics also follow the contour of the line.

e.g.   1)

2)

3) Identify the smaller motifs or phrases. Note the structural connectives such as phrase groupings, statements of themes, rhythmic sequences, melodic repetitions.

4) As a phrase is analogous to a sentence, remember to accentuate the words (notes) which convey the meaning. Emphasize the fundamental tones as defined by the harmonic structure and relate the other tones proportionately.

Excerpt from Concertino

Chaminade

e.g.

4) Determine the relative importance of the phrase in the overall musical context and place it accordingly: is it a solo line, countermelody, or accompanimental figure.

In every composition there will be a thread of continuity which should be observed and sustained. It is this structure, no matter how aleatory or culturally biased, that separates music from noise. Strive to project beyond the technical notation and convey a meaningful interpretation with the use of appropriate nuances.

ARTICULATION

Articulation is the pronunciation of a musical sound which involves the starting, duration, and release of the sound. Appropriate nuances of articulation should aid in the flow of the musical line, and give character and meaning to otherwise monotonous note patterns.

Types of Attack

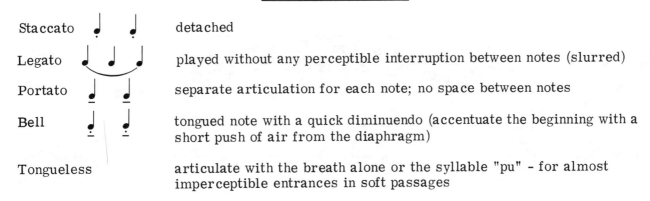

Staccato	detached
Legato	played without any perceptible interruption between notes (slurred)
Portato	separate articulation for each note; no space between notes
Bell	tongued note with a quick diminuendo (accentuate the beginning with a short push of air from the diaphragm)
Tongueless	articulate with the breath alone or the syllable "pu" - for almost imperceptible entrances in soft passages

Duration

Articulation patterns determine the manner in which notes are emphasized throughout each phrase. As a general rule, a slur over a group of notes emphasizes the first note beneath the slur.

e.g.:

Note: Meter and tempo also indicate the relative intensity of stress placed upon note groups.

Types of release

martelé	⊐	abrupt ending
resonant	◡	release with a lifting of the breath
fade-out	▷	gradually lessen flow of air until the tone no longer sounds

DAILY STUDIES

"Genius at first is little more than a great capacity for receiving discipline."

Major Scales

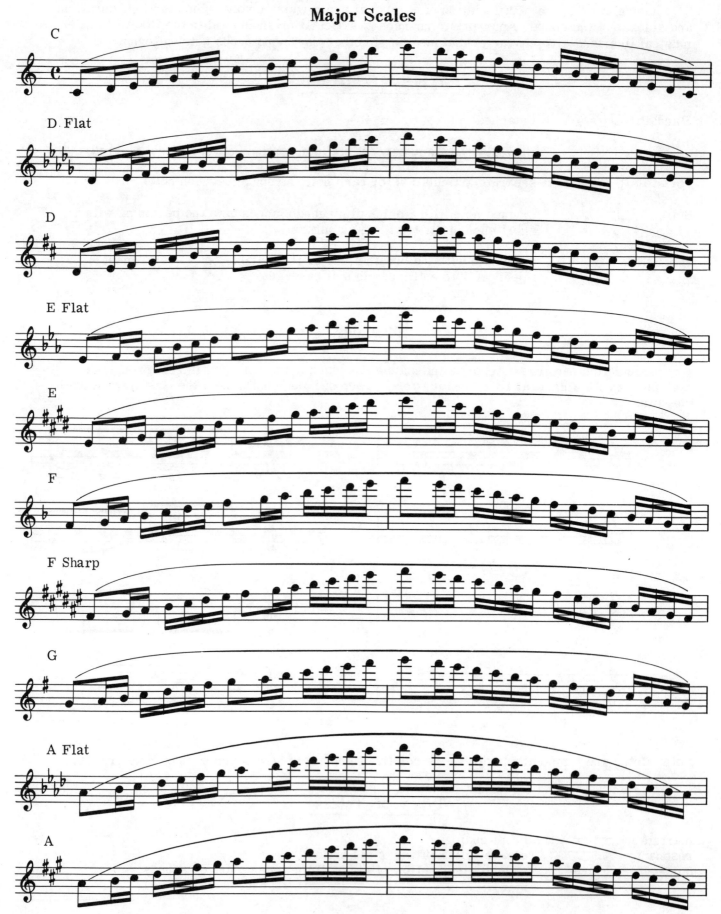

B Flat

B

Natural Minor Scales

Cm

C#m

Dm

Ebm

Em

Fm

F#m

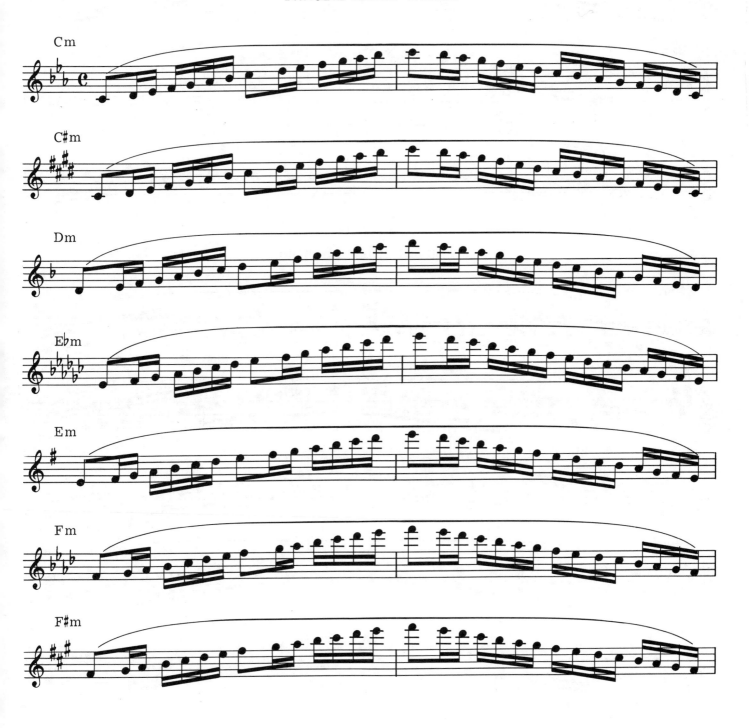

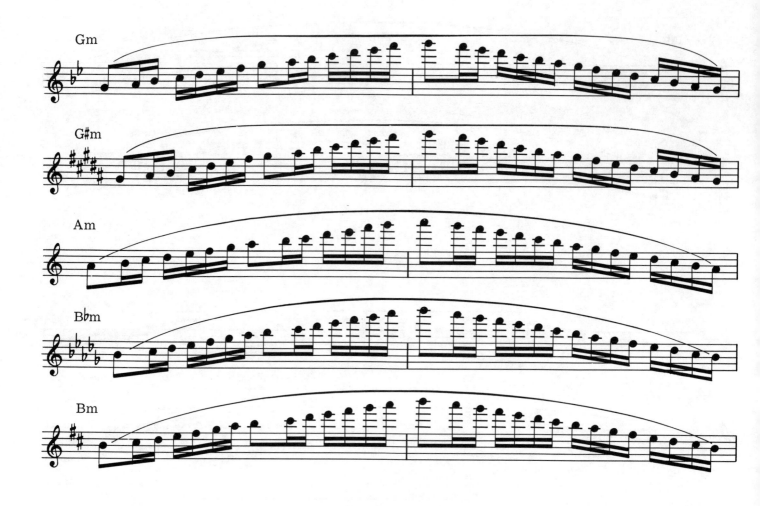

Harmonic Minor Scales

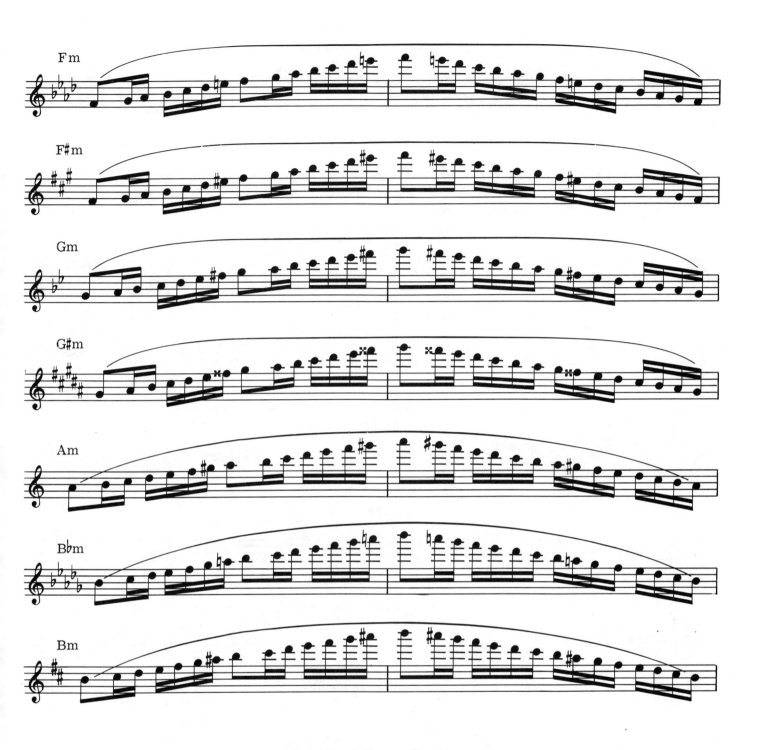

Melodic Minor Scales

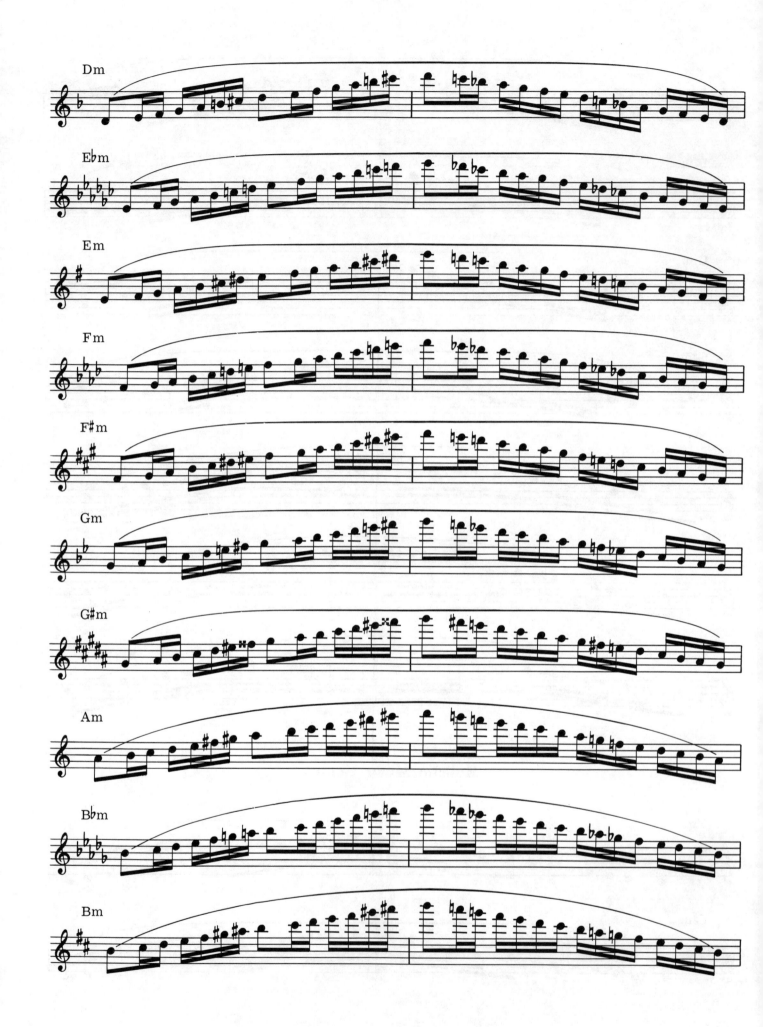

Chromatic Scale

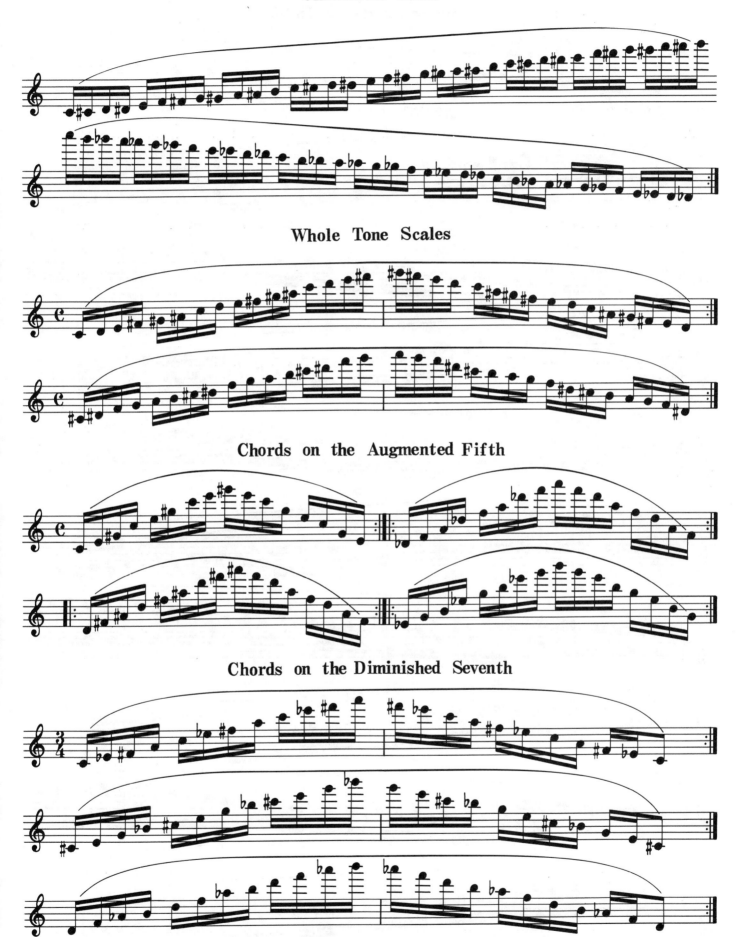

Whole Tone Scales

Chords on the Augmented Fifth

Chords on the Diminished Seventh

Major Scales in Thirds

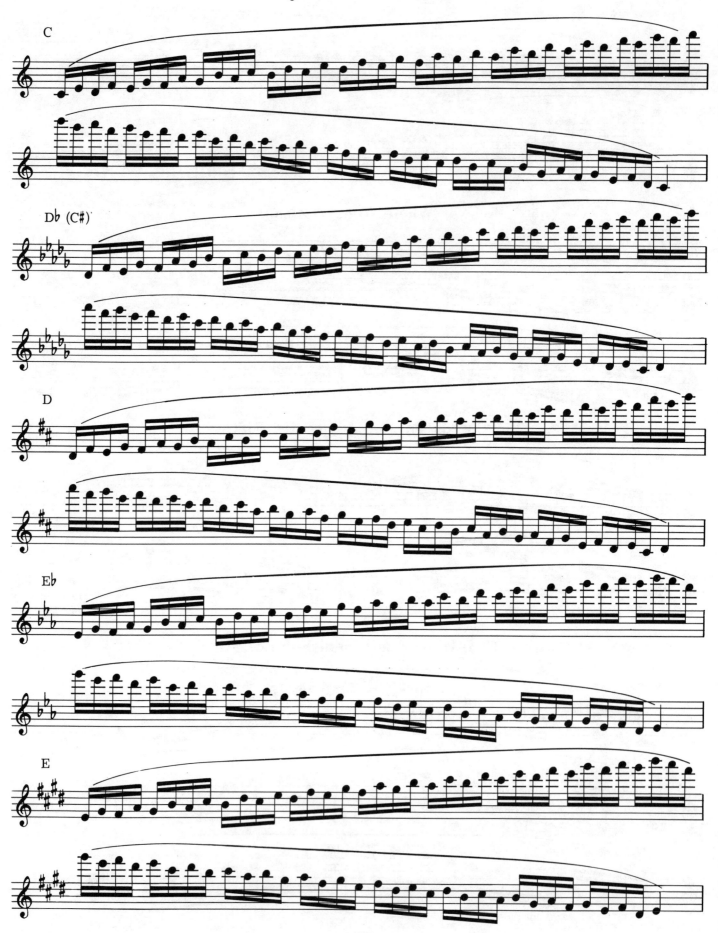

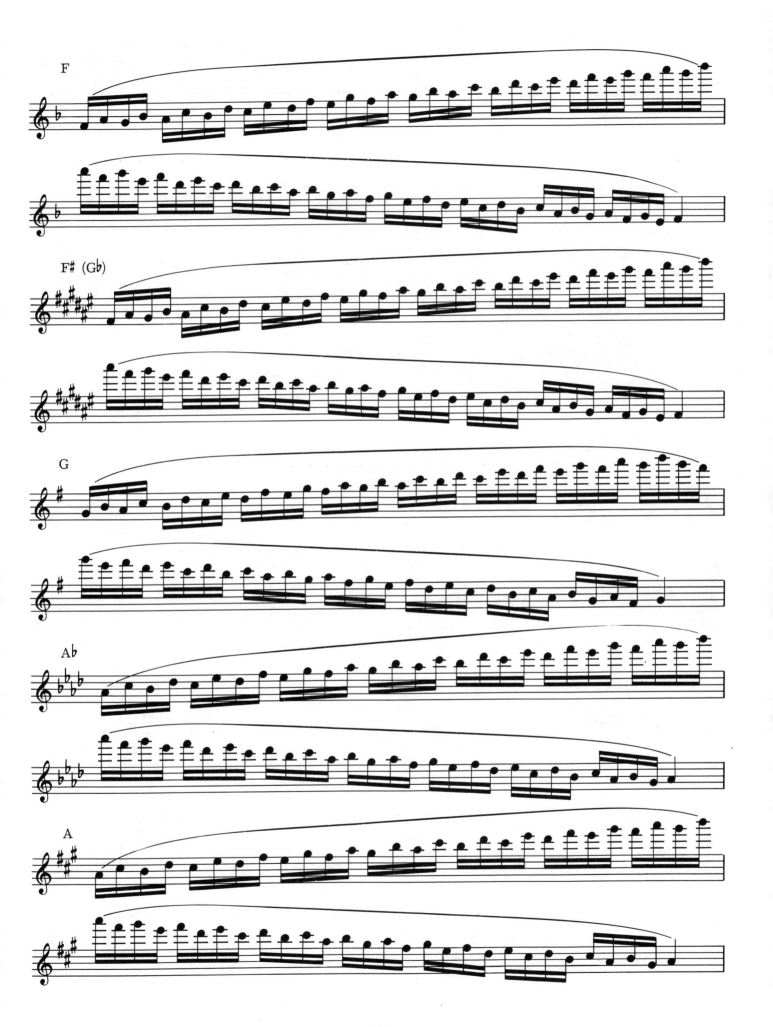

73

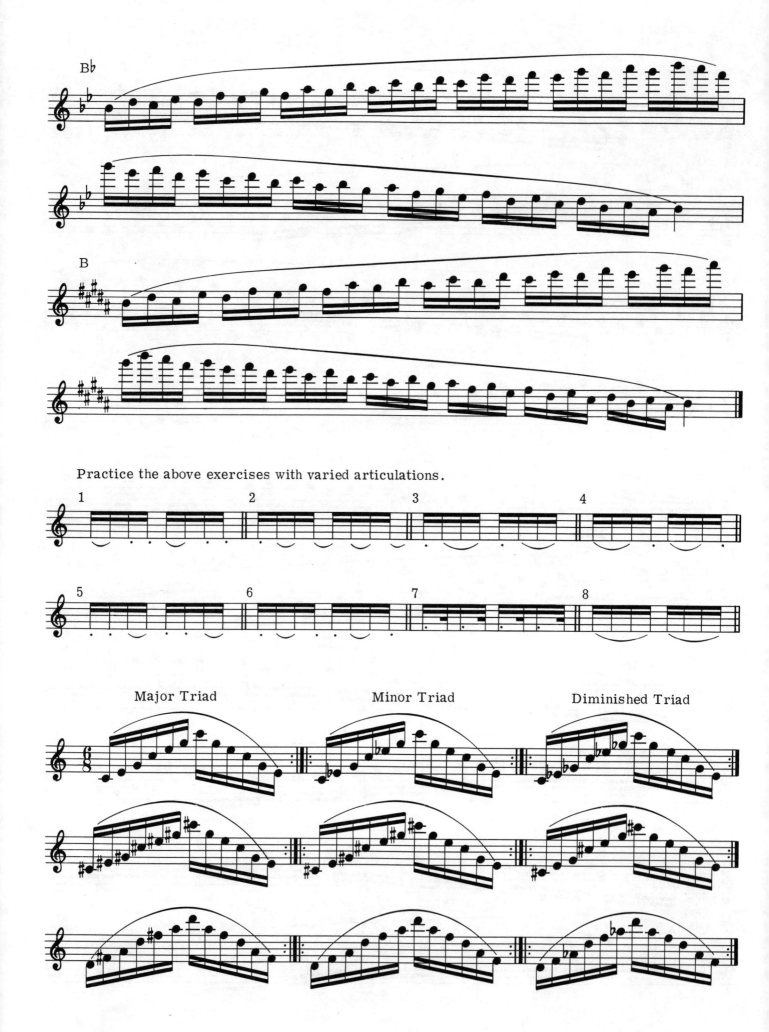

Practice the above exercises with varied articulations.

Major Triad   Minor Triad   Diminished Triad

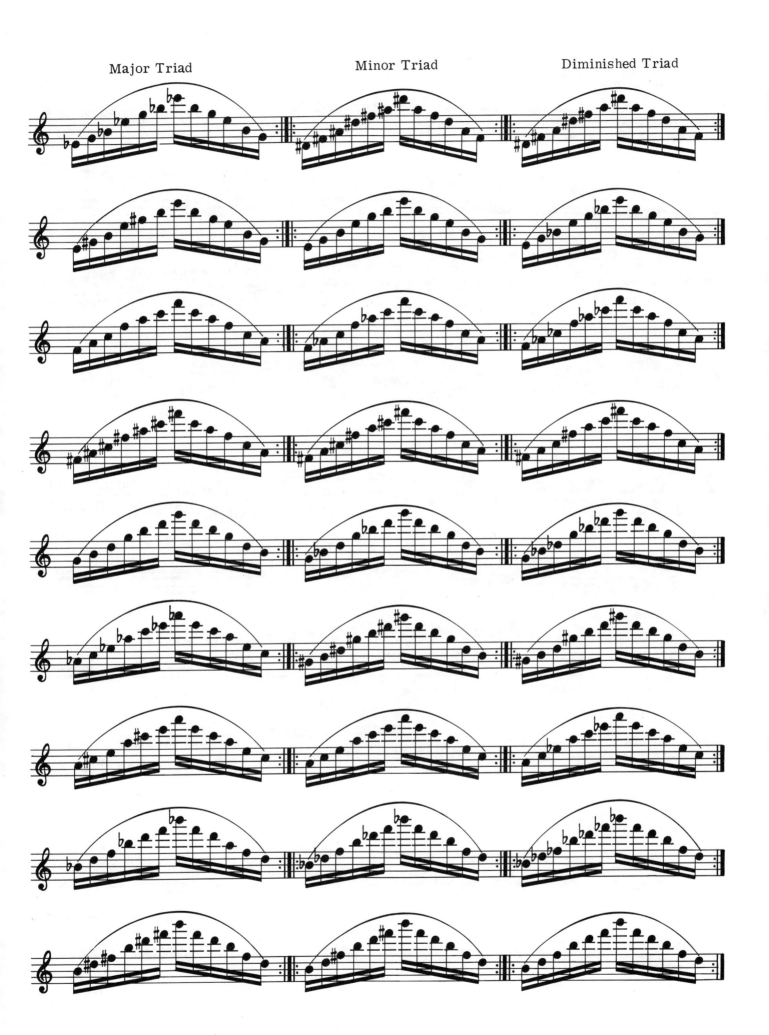

Major Seconds

Minor Thirds

Major Thirds

Perfect Fourths

Tritones

Perfect Fifths

Minor Sixths

Major Sixths

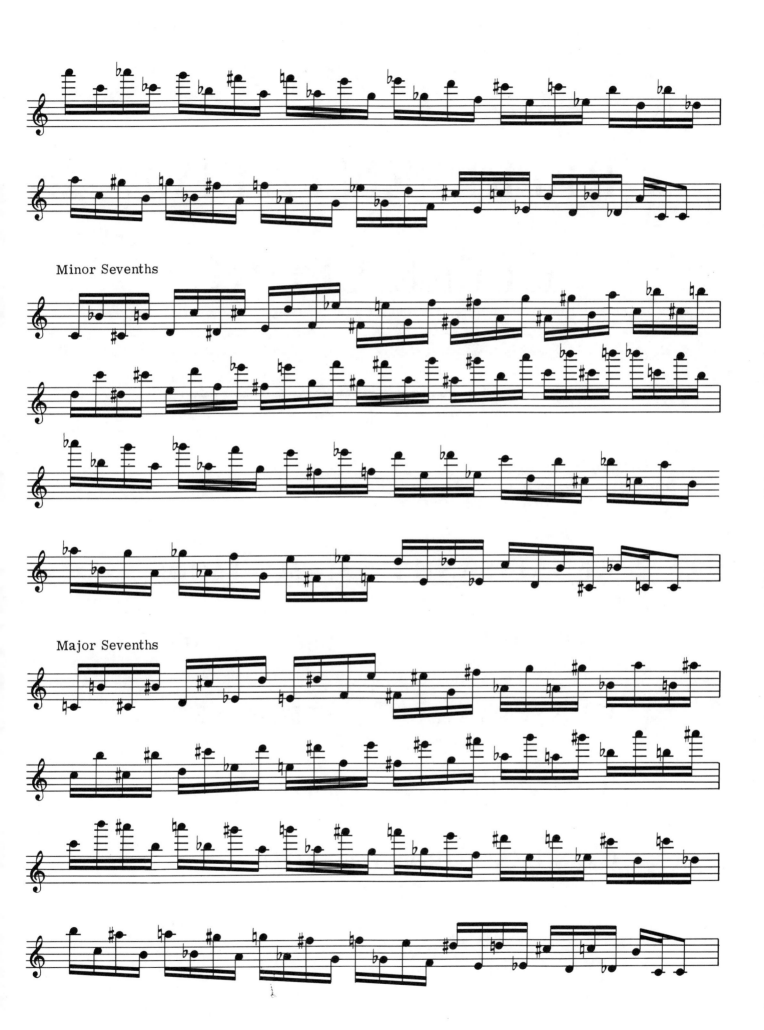

Minor Sevenths

Major Sevenths

REPRESENTATIVE
LITERATURE

RENAISSANCE	1450 - 1600
BAROQUE	1600 - 1750
CLASSICAL	1750 - 1820
ROMANTIC	1820 - 1900
CONTEMPORARY	1900 -

RENAISSANCE ERA 1450-1600

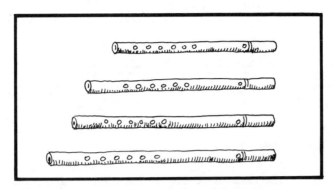

from Martin Agricola, <u>Musica</u> <u>instrumentalis</u> <u>deudsch</u> (1529)

INSTRUMENTS:

Sixteenth century literature supports the existence of a consort of flutes. Typically these instruments were pitched a fifth apart (g, d', a') with each having a range of more than two octaves. They were made of wood, had a cylindrical bore (occasionally in two sections), six finger holes, and an embouchure hole. These flutes fingered a diatonic scale but could play chromatically by half-holing.

TIME FRAME AND USAGE:

Instrumental music of the Renaissance was usually transcribed from vocal works. Consorts resembled vocal ensembles with four or more parts ranging from bass to soprano. As instruments of the time were limited in range and flexibility, a consort of instruments in each family was needed to cover an extended range. Dynamic contrast occurred when loud wind consorts alternated with softer string consorts. With much of the music being performed in large churches, reverberant acoustical properties permitted few nuances of articulation and only the use of longer note values. Two types of textures were employed in this era:

1) interweaving solo melodic lines based on modal scales
2) succession of chords resulting from the combination of melodic lines

Common instrumental forms of the period included: the dance (pavane and galliard, ronde and salterello), fantasias, ricercares, canzonas, variations, and grounds. Although few instrumental works call specifically for the flute, its resemblance to the recorder allows the interchange of literature between the two.

<u>Stylistic</u> <u>features</u> <u>of</u> <u>Renaissance</u> <u>music</u>

1) little dynamic change
2) long note values
3) few nuances of attack and release
4) no vibrato

LA GIRANDOLA

Thomas Morley (1557-1602)

BAROQUE ERA 1600-1750

Flute-maker/performer/composer Hotteterre is credited with the development of the one-keyed flute. It emerged as early as 1670 and its features included:

1) construction in three sections - smaller sections allowed for easier construction and tuning
2) cylindrical headjoint and conical body (tapering towards the foot joint)
3) addition of a D♯ key (seventh finger hole)
4) usually made of hardwoods or ivory

In the 1720's the one-keyed flute was further refined when the middle joint was divided into two sections (each having three finger holes). Interchangeable joints called corps de rechange were used to change pitch as needed. Other devices used to compensate for pitch changes included: an adjustable headjoint stopper, and an addition of a telescoping section of tube to the foot joint (called a register).

TIME FRAME AND USAGE:

During the Baroque Era most familiar forms of instrumental music emerged; the sonata, trio-sonata, concerto, concerto grosso, fugue, dance suite or partita (allemande, courante, sarabande, gigue), overture, et al. A solo instrument with a supporting bass and accompanimental middle parts gradually took the place of the instrumental consort. Harmonic theory and figured bass came about and major/minor tonalities replaced older church modes. Instrumental pieces were based upon a unifying motive or the repeated statement of a fugue. Simple melodic lines were treated contrapuntally and extensively ornamented for added expression.

Stylistic features of Baroque music

1) moderate dynamic contrast from p to f (use of terraced or blocked dynamics)
2) crescendo and diminuendo used sparingly
3) little use of vibrato as we know it - use of "flattement" or vibrato made by the finger shaking over the open tone hole
4) extensive ornamentation added by performer as a principle means of expression

BAROQUE ORNAMENTATION

While it is now common for ornaments to be written in the music, composers of the Baroque Era frequently notated only a skeletal melody which was to be freely embellished by the performer. Consequently, the interpretation of a piece varied with each performance. Today, however, the practice of editing original (urtext) manuscripts has made it convenient for the performer to add appropriate ornamentation.

In the interest of authenticity there are excellent sources which discuss the original practice of embellishing the unadorned line. There are two sources of particular interest to the flutist. One is a treatise by the mid-eighteenth century musician J.J. Quantz. His <u>On Flute Playing</u> devotes entire sections to the practice of performing essential ornaments. The other is a set of <u>Twelve Methodical Sonatas, Op. 13</u> by G.P. Telemann. These were written for the study of ornamentation as Telemann wrote a suggested line of embellishment below the simplified melodic line of each slow movement.

e.g.:

Excerpt from Sonata No. 1 in g minor

G.P. Telemann

The refined skill of ornamenting in the Baroque style requires knowledge, experience, and musical sensitivity, all of which come through practice and thoughtful study. For additional information on Baroque performance practices see:

R. Donington, The Interpretation of Early Music, London, 1974.
J. Hotteterre, Rudiments of the Flute, Recorder, and Oboe, N.Y. 1968. (or pub. 1707).
B.B. Mather and D. Lasocki, Free Ornamentation in Woodwind Music 1770-1775, N.Y. 1976.
B.B. Mather, Interpretation of French Music from 1675 to 1775, N.Y., 1973.
J. Veilhan, The Rules of Musical Interpretation in the Baroque, Paris, 1979.

The following chart outlines some of the more common symbols used in the notation of ornaments:

ECOS
for unaccompanied flute

from Premier livre de pieces pour la flûte traversière

Jacques Hotteterre (1680-1761)

CLASSICAL ERA 1750-1820

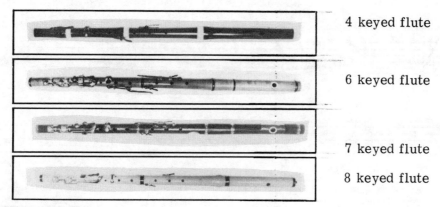

4 keyed flute

6 keyed flute

7 keyed flute

8 keyed flute

INSTRUMENTS:

In the mid 18th century the need for technical facility inspired instrument makers to experiment with additional keys. To further eliminate half-holing and cross fingerings three more keys were added to the flute:

1) an F key (between the two lowest tone holes)
2) a G# key (operated by the left little finger)
3) a B flat key for the left thumb

Extensions of the 4 keyed flute were the 6 and 8 keyed flutes.
6 keyed flute: low C and C# keys were added to the foot joint
8 keyed flute: 1) additional c" key (operated by the first finger of the r.h.)
          2) alternate long F key (operated by the left little finger)

Three, five, and seven key variations of the above existed but were never as common as the eight keyed flute.

TIME FRAME AND USAGE:

Elaborate contrapuntal styles of the Baroque were generally abandoned in the Classical Era. Instrumental music of the time showed restraint of emotional extremes, objectivism, refinement, clarity of form, and structural discipline. Melodies were set against simple accompaniments and treatment of thematic, harmonic, and rhythmic material was both logical and predictable. Ornamentation was used judiciously and almost exclusively at cadence points. Sonata and concerto forms were favored, the latter employing the use of the cadenza - a passage in which the instrumentalist displayed technical facility by improvising a brilliant virtuosic solo.

Stylistic features of Classical music

1) dynamic range from p to f
2) ornamentation reduced to the trill, turn, and mordent - composers preferred to write out their own stylistic interpretation
3) staccato introduced
4) careful, clean execution demanded of performers
5) vibrato used sparingly
6) emphasis on beauty of tone

from Six Duo Concertans pour Deux Flutes

Anton Stamitz
(1754 1809)

Menuetto
Con Var.

Var. 2

Var.3

98

ROMANTIC ERA 1820-1900

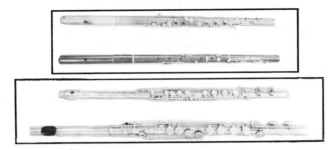

Boehm conical flutes

Boehm flutes after 1847

INSTRUMENTS:

In the mid 19th century a craftsman/musician named Theobald Boehm began to refine the flute mechanism. His early experimentation led to the introduction of several conical flutes. Their features included:
1) enlarged tone holes for a more powerful sound
2) repositioned tone holes for improved intonation
3) ring key mechanism - allowing one finger to operate other keys while closing its own
4) horizontal rod axles - for connecting keys
5) more logical fingering system - use of consecutive finger motion for the chromatic scale (inclusion of an open g♯ key)

While Boehm was responsible for many innovations, other instrument makers contributed to modifications in the Boehm system:
1) Auguste Buffet - repositioned the rod axles and developed a mechanically useful "clutch" mechanism
2) Victor Coche - added a C♯/D♯ till key for the 3rd finger r.h.
3) Vincent Dorus - devised an arrangement for a return to the closed g♯ key (a holdover from fingering systems on earlier flutes)

In 1847 Boehm introduced yet another flute which revolutionized flute design. His design of 1847 remains the basic pattern (with a few modifications) followed by instrument makers today. Its features included:
1) cylindrical tube/parabolic head joint (tapering in a curve towards the stopper)
2) larger tone holes (necessitating the use of padded key covers)
3) improved intonation through acoustically correct positioning of keys
4) use of metal (silver) for unsurpassed tonal brilliance
5) enlarged embouchure hole and additional lip plate to aid in production of a stronger tone and assist in direction of breath

Later changes in the Boehm system included:
1) Clair Godefroy and Louis Lot's perforated finger plates-"French open-hole"
2) Giulio Briccialdi's B flat thumb mechanism

TIME FRAME AND USAGE:

Nineteenth century Romanticism departed from the constraints of the Classical Era. A great diversity of styles emerged reflecting a new individualism, emotionalism, subjectivism, and nationalism. Harmonic idioms expanded and strayed from strict major/minor tonalities. Chromaticism was used extensively as well as new chord progressions, altered chords, non-harmonic tones, tonal obscurity, and modulation for effect. Formal structures were allowed a greater freedom. Classical sonatas and concerti were replaced by the fantasy, nocturne, ballad, arabesque, romance, and a host of other descriptive, and programmatic titles. Wind instrument technology was vastly improved. Elaborate practice etudes exploiting technical mastery were concertized and the virtuoso performer came into his own.

Stylistic features of Romantic music

1) extremes of dynamic range - ppp to fff
2) use of sudden dynamic changes
3) stylistic, tempo, and dynamic markings used by composers
4) extensive use of vibrato for expression and tone coloring
5) numerous types of articulation employed

Air Varié pour la Flûte

During the 19th centruy a great number of composers favored the use of the air varie or theme and variations. Technological improvements of the flute mechanism inspired the composition of these showy pieces. Although today they are considered to be lesser works, they were once popular as a vehicle for the display of technical virtuosity.

Jean Louis Tulou
(1786-1865)

Poco Adagio cantabile

Var. 1
Poco più animato

Var. 2
Poco più lento

Var. 3

Fine

CHANT D'AMOUR.
(A Love Song.)

As to the flow'ret the sun is pleasure,
As to lily the calm blue stream;
Thou art my life's rich treasure
My bliss supreme.

Carl Reinecke
(1824-1910)

102

CHANT D'AMOUR

Carl Reinecke
(1824–1910)

104

CONTEMPORARY MUSIC

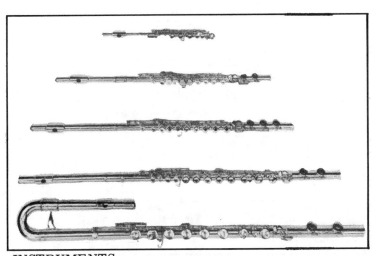

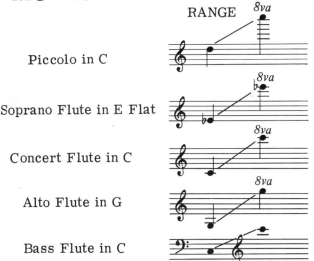

RANGE

Piccolo in C

Soprano Flute in E Flat

Concert Flute in C

Alto Flute in G

Bass Flute in C

INSTRUMENTS:

Beyond standard Boehm models flute makers now offer a variety of extra key options to facilitate playing: open G♯ key (in original Boehm design), low B foot, French open hole, reversed B♭ thumb, B-C trill, C♯ trill (aids in trill from high G to A), split E (facilitates playing high E), low C♯ roller, low E♭ roller, B♭ - F♯ mechanism (allows playing F♯ and B without sliding left thumb from the B♭ lever), high C gizmo (operates low B key to facilitate playing the highest C).

Contemporary flute designers have attempted to improve pitch irregularities of the Boehm flute. Resulting options now available to the flutist include: the Coltman C♯ key, Cooper scale, revised Armstrong scale, William Bennett scale. The search for improved sonority and response has resulted in:
1) use of high density metals for enriched sound (platinum, gold, silver)
2) undercutting (fraizing) tone holes and embouchure holes for more efficient response in all registers
3) replacement of cork stopper with "O"-Ring for greater resonance.

Flute design is an ongoing process. Widespread acceptance and production of the Boehm flute is seemingly immune to changing fashion, however, this does not eliminate the need for further changes or improvements in design.

TIME FRAME AND USAGE:

The Contemporary idiom encompasses a variety of styles. Although highly diversified, broad stylistic trends have included: neoromanticism (heavy emotionalism), impressionism (experimentation with tone coloring), expressionism (subjective, dissonant, atonal), and neo-classicism (revived contrapuntalism, simplicity, clarity of form). The twentieth century has witnessed a radical departure from conventional major/minor tonalities. New concepts of tonality include: multitonality (numerous keys used consecutively), microtonality (division of the octave into more than twelve notes), polytonality (use of several keys simultaneously), and atonality (negation of any tonality). Rhythm and meter have undergone a similar expansion to include: nonmetric music (improvisatory), multimetric music (frequent changes of meter), and polymetric music (two or more different meters employed simultaneously). Contemporary idioms further expand sonorities by unusual manipulation of conventional instruments (buzzing into woodwinds, clicking keys, humming while playing). Sonorities have also been enhanced with the aid of electronic devices: tapes, amplifiers, filters, oscillators, synthesizers.

Stylistic features of Contemporary music

1) extended range of instruments (altissimo registers, microtones)
2) full range of dynamics (barely audible - threshold of pain)
3) separation of sound into its elements (pure sound as an end in itself)
4) special effects (multiphonics, harmonics, electronic modulation, etc.)

HIGH REGISTER/CONTEMPORARY NOTATION

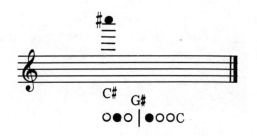

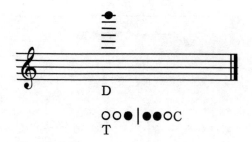

Chromatic Exercise

Contemporary Notation

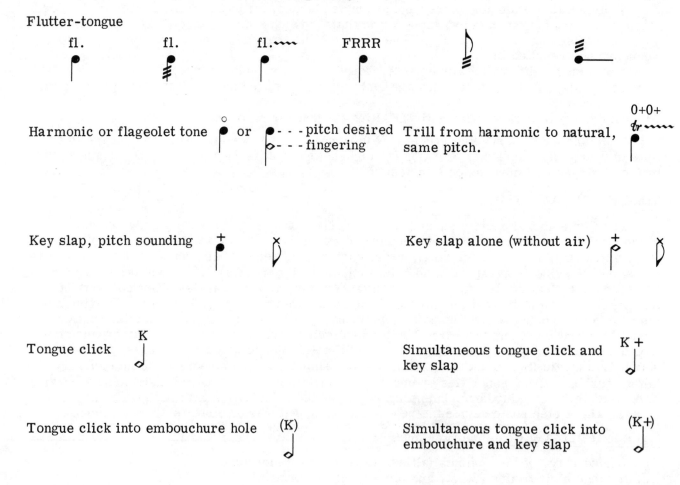

CONTEMPORARY NOTATION

Whistle/whisper tone (WT)

- - - - whistle tone sounding
- - - - fingering
WS.

Simultaneous playing and singing

or

- - - -played pitch   - - - -played pitch
S - - - -sung pitch   x - - - -sung pitch

Simultaneous playing and humming

- - - - hummed pitch
- - - - played pitch

Glissando: ⌐⌐ or ⌐∿⌐

Bending-rolling flute inward
and lipping downward

bend

Jet whistle   ⌐ approximate pitch
- - - - fingering

Proportional rhythm:

As rapidly as possible

Accelerando

Ritardando

Jet whistle/air rush-loud exhalation through flute,
lips around embouchure

Jet whistle/air rush-loud inhalation through flute,
lips around embouchure

Vibrato
   Nonvibrato   nv
   Normal vibrato   V

Key vibrato (KV)

Tongue without pitch   V V V

Flutter-tongue without sound.   r

Pitch variation:
   Slightly sharp ↑   Slightly flat ↓

   Almost 1/4 tone sharp ⬆   Almost 1/4 tone flat ⬇

Rattle keys without blowing x   x

"He who sets limits for himself will always be expected to remain within them."

R. Schumann

Opus I

SELECTED REPERTOIRE LIST

*For Unaccompanied Flute
Composer

Work(s)

Albinoni, Tomaso (1671-1751)
Arnold, Malcolm (1921-)
Bach, Carl Philipp Emanuel (1714-1788)

Bach, Johann Sebastian (1685-1750)

Beck, John Ness (1930-)
Beethoven, Ludwig van (1770-1827)
Benda, Franz (1709-1786)
Berio, Luciano (1925-)
Bizet, Georges (1838-1875)
Blavet, Michel (1700-1768)
Bloch, Ernest (1880-1959)
Boccherini, Luigi (1743-1805)
Boulez, Pierre (1925-)
Bournoville, Armand (1805-1879)
Bozza, Eùgene (1905-)
Briccaldi, Giulio (1818-1881)
Burton, Eldin (1913-)
Busser, Henri (1872-1973)
Caplet, André (1878-1925)
Chaminade, Cécile (1857-1944)
Chopin, Frédéric (1810-1849)
Copland, Aaron (1900-)
Dahl, Ingolf (1912-1970)
David, Thomas (1925-)
Davidovsky, Mario (1934-)
Debussy, Claude (1862-1918)
Doppler, Franz (1821-1883)
Dutilleux, Henri (1916-)
Enesco, Georges (1881-1955)
Fauré, Gabriel (1845-1924)
Frederick II (the Great) (1712-1786)
Ganne, Louis (1862-1923)
Gaubert, Philippe (1879-1941)
Genzmer, Harald (1909-)
Gluck, Christoph Willibald (1714-1787)
Godard, Benjamin (1849-1895)
Goldman, Richard Franko (1910-)
Grétry, André Modeste (1741-1813)
Griffes, Charles T. (1884-1920)
Handel, George Frederick (1685-1759)
Hanson, Howard (1896-1981)
Haydn, Franz Joseph (1732-1809)
Hindemith, Paul (1895-1963)
Hoffmeister, Franz Anton (1754-1812)
Honegger, Arthur (1892-1955)
Hue, Georges (1858-1948)
Ibert, Jacques (1890-1962)

Sonata in a, Op. 6, #6, Concerto in G
*Fantasy for Flute Solo
*Sonata in a
Six Sonatas, Concerti in G, A, a, B♭
*Partita in a
Six Sonatas, Suite in b
Sonata
Serenade, Op. 41
Sonatas in F, e, G
Sequenza
Menuet from L'Arlésienne, Suite #2
Six Sonatas, Op. 2, Six Sonatas, Op. 3
Suite Modale (1956)
Concerto In D
Sonatine (1946)
Danse Pour Katia
*Image
Carnival of Venice
Concerto, Sonatina
Prelude et Scherzo, Op. 35
Réverie and Petite Valse, Improvisation
Concertino
Variations on a Theme by Rossini
Duo for Flute and Piano
*Variations on a Swedish Folktune (1945)
*Sonata (1951)
Synchronisms (1963) for Flute and Tape
Syrinx
Fantasie Pastorale Hongroise, Op. 26
Sonatine
Cantabile et Presto
Fantasie, Op. 79
Sonatas, Concerti
Andante et Scherzo
Nocturne et Allegro Scherzando, Madrigal
*Sonata for Solo Flute
Dance of the Blessed Spirits
Suite, Op. 116
*Two Monochromes
Concerto in C
Poem
Ten Sonatas
Serenade
Concerto in D
Sonata, *Acht Stücke, Echo
Concerto in D, G
*Danse De La Chevre
Fantasie
*Piéce, Concerto
Jeux-Sonatine

Composer	Work(s)
Jacob, Gordon (b.1895-)	Concerto
Jacobi, Frederick (1891-1952)	Night Piece and Dance
Kennan, Kent (1913-)	Night Soliloquy
Latham, William (1917-)	Sonata #2, Suite in Baroque Style
Leclair, Jean Marie (1697-1764)	Sonatas in C, b, e, G, Concerto in C
Locatelli, Pietro (1695-1764)	Sonatas in F, G, D, g
Loeillet, Jean Baptiste (1680-1730)	Twelve Sonatas, Op. 2, Six Sonatas, Op. 3, Op. 1, 3 Sonatas
Marcello, Benedetto (1686-1739)	Sonatas, Op. 2
Martin, Frank (1890-1974)	Ballade
Martinu, Bohuslav (1890-1959)	First Sonata (1945)
Messiaen, Olivier (1908-)	Le Merle Noir
Milhaud, Darius (1892-1974)	Sonatine (1922)
Moevs, Robert (1920-)	*Pan
Molique, Wilhelm Bernhard (1802-1869)	Concerto in d
Mozart, Wolfgang Amadeus (1756-1791)	Six Sonatas, K. 10-15, Concerti in G,D,C
Muczynski, Robert (1929-)	Sonata, Op. 14
Nielson, Carl A. (1865-1931)	Concerto
Paganini, Nicolò (1782-1840)	24 Caprices
Pergolesi, Giovanni B. (1710-1736)	Concerti in D, G
Persichetti, Vincent (1915-)	*Parable
Pessard, Emile (1843-1917)	Andalouse
Piston, Walter (1894-1976)	Sonata
Poulenc, Francis (1899-1963)	Sonata
Prokofieff, Sergey (1891-1953)	Sonata in D, Op. 94
Quantz, Johann Joachim (1697-1773)	Concerti in G, e
Reinecke, Karl (1824-1910)	Sonata "Undine", Op. 167
Rivier, Jean (b.1896-)	Concerto for Flute and Orchestra
Roussel, Albert (1869-1937)	Joueurs de Flûte, Op. 27, Andante et Scherzo, Op. 51
Saint-Saëns, Camille (1835-1921)	Air de Ballet
Schubert, Franz (1797-1828)	Introduction and Variations, Op. 160
Telemann, Georg Philipp (1681-1767)	Suite in a, Sonatas, *Twelve Fantasias
Tomasi, Henri (1901-1971)	Concerto in F
Varése, Edgar (1883-1965)	*Density 21.5
Vaughan Williams, Ralph (1872-1958)	Suite de Ballet
Vivaldi, Antonio (1678-1741)	Concerti, Sonatas
Widor, Charles Marie (1844-1937)	Suite, Op. 34
Wilder, Alec (1907-)	Sonata (1965)

For a thorough, annotated listing of flute repertoire see:

Pellerite, James J. A Handbook of Literature for the Flute. 3rd ed., rev. Bloomington, In.: Zalo Publications, 1978.

For a thorough listing of all categories of published flute music (combination ensembles) see:

Vester, Frans, (ed.). Flute Repertoire Catalogue: 10,000 Titles. London: Musica Rara, 1967.